Alcohol Awarness Manual

1844252957

Haynes

Alcohol
Manual

Gaylin Tudhope
Cartoons by Jim Campbell

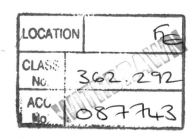
© Gaylin Tudhope 2006

Haynes Publishing
Sparkford, Yeovil, Somerset BA22 7JJ, England

Haynes North America, Inc
861 Lawrence Drive, Newbury Park, California 91320, USA

Editions Haynes
4, Rue de l'Abreuvoir
92415 COURBEVOIE CEDEX, France

Haynes Publishing Nordiska AB
Box 1504, 751 45 Uppsala, Sweden

British Library Cataloguing in Publication Data:
A catalogue record for this book is available from the British Library

ISBN-10: 1 84425 295 4
ISBN-13: 978 1 84425 295 4

Printed in Britain by J. H. Haynes & Co. Ltd., Sparkford.

The Author and the Publisher have taken care to ensure that the advice given in this edition is current at the time of publication. The Reader is advised to read and understand the instructions and information material included with all medicines recommended, and to consider carefully the appropriateness of any treatments. The Author and the Publisher will have no liability for adverse results, inappropriate or excessive use of the remedies offered in this book or their level of effectiveness in individual cases. The Author and the Publisher do not intend that this book be used as a substitute for medical advice. Advice from a medical practitioner should always be sought for any symptom or illness.

Illustration and photo credits:
Front cover photos © iStockphoto.com (Auke Holwerds, Jim Jurica, Laura Tomlinson, Lisa F Young, Lise Gagne).

Other iStockphoto images as marked.

Haynes photos courtesy of Bob Jex, Carole Turk, Em Willmott, Paul Buckland and Tracey Robertson.

Illustrations by Jim Campbell, Mark Stevens, Matthew Marke and Roger Healing.

Contents

Author's acknowledgements

In the making of this book I fear I might have turned a number of people to drink. My support team have been invaluable, not only in keeping me sane but in actually helping to create a readable work. For encouragement and help with the book my thanks go to Jeff Balderson and Jean Rober, and for moral support to my two long-suffering children Matthew and Aislinn. Thanks also to J. Haynes for the original idea, to Matthew Minter who has stoically guided me through all the expectations and nuts and bolts of creation, to Dr. Simon Gregory for his reading of the text, and to the rest of the team at Haynes who have helped turn what was just a bucket of parts into a working and functioning engine.

Introduction

The substance we call alcohol is made using a process known as fermentation, where yeast breaks down sugar into alcohol and carbon dioxide. This reaction is caused by the yeast itself, which is simply a fungus that contains enzymes which complete this process. As the fermentation proceeds, the carbon dioxide disperses out, leaving a mixture of alcohol and water. This process is used to make beers, lagers and wines. If a stronger alcoholic drink – such as rum, vodka, etc – is desired, distillation is required. In this second process, the water-alcohol mixture is heated to a vapour, then cooled so that it condenses into a more concentrated version, leaving the bulk of the water behind.

You will have heard of fermentation in relation to other things besides the making of alcoholic beverages. What about bread making? Yeast is mixed with the bread dough, then is left in a warm place to rise. In this case it is the carbon dioxide produced by the yeast that causes the bread to rise. Very little alcohol is produced, and what there is will mostly be destroyed in the baking process.

The Czechs are known to consume the most beer per person in the world. And there is a Czech proverb which says, 'Value water, but drink wine.'

Photo: © iStockphoto.com, John Kerher

What about yogurt? That is also created through fermentation. However, unlike bread and alcohol, the fermentation is introduced not by yeast, but by bacteria.

Pickles, anyone? The pickled cucumber, or rather the vinegar in which it is pickled, is also made through the method of fermentation. Like yogurt, this too uses bacteria for fermenting rather than yeast, though the starting point in this case is a liquid containing some alcohol! (The word vinegar comes from the French *vin aîgre*, meaning sour wine.) So the process of fermentation can produce a variety of food and drink.

Despite the problems it can cause, alcohol is not necessarily an evil to be avoided. It is only as evil as the drinker allows it to be. Drinking in moderation can be an enjoyable activity. It is when alcohol is consumed in great quantities and/or for extended periods of time that it affects the drinker adversely. The main thing to remember is if you drink at all, do so only in moderation and never while driving or in the workplace.

In this book, the term alcohol has mostly been used to refer to the drinking kind. However, there are other uses and different types of alcohol as well. Some kinds of alcohol – as methanol and ethanol – can be burned for fuel. (In Brazil it is known as gasohol, and is more common than petrol.) Also, ethanol – which is the least toxic of alcohols – is used in making perfumes and colognes. It prevents the plant and animal extracts in the perfumes from wearing off.

Ethanol is also the type of alcohol used in flavourings such as vanilla extract. In this instance, it is used to dissolve chemicals that are otherwise difficult or impossible to dissolve in water. Finally, ethanol with a small amount of methanol added is used in cleaning products. The methanol is highly poisonous, thus making it unsafe to consume, which accounts for the warning labels on those products which contain it.

Stressed within these pages is the fact that if you are driving, you should not be drinking – **at all**. If drinking don't drive – **at all**. Plan your drinking when you go out beforehand so you can designate a person to drive who has had no alcohol. Even light to moderate drinking will affect a person's response time when driving, as well as their driving skills. The same goes for operating machinery and power tools, whether at work or at home. And although you can't be disqualified for it, drinking and cycling is a pretty bad idea too.

Drinking alcohol affects blood sugar levels. What does this mean? It means that drinking alcohol may make you feel hungry. If this happens, often there is only junk food available. Junk food generally refers to foods with low nutritional value. If you find that you are eating those foods while drinking, you may be consuming more calories and fat than you realise. Think about what you tend to eat while drinking. Do any of these foods look familiar?

- One-third of a pizza supreme contains 14 grams of fat.
- A burrito with beans and cheese contains 188 calories.
- A plain hamburger contains 275 calories and 17 grams of fat.
- A hot dog contains 242 calories and over 14 grams of fat.
- A plain cheeseburger contains 320 calories and more than 15 grams of fat.
- A typical portion of chips contains 235 calories and 12 grams of fat.
- A typical sub sandwich contains 456 calories and over 18 grams of fat.

Some kinds of alcohol are used as biofuel

H44842

For a list of the healthiest fast foods, check out
www.fatfreekitchen.com/junkfoods/healthy-fast-foods.html

Don't allow your alcohol consumption to influence your choices
in foods. Choose wisely when you eat, and always eat while
drinking, if possible. It will help you drink less and stay on the
pathway to moderate or controlled drinking.

While we know that drinking alcohol to excess can be
detrimental to our health, we also know that alcohol in moderate
amounts can actually be beneficial. For adult men and women,
having a drink or two daily may help prevent heart disease. The
sad fact is, many people tend to drink too much, ultimately
increasing the risk to their health. If your aim is to consume two
units per day (see *Just what is a 'drink' and what is a 'unit'* on
page 13) and you skip a few days, do not try to 'make up for it'
on the weekend. Binge drinking is definitely bad for your health.
It can result in coma or even death. It is always better to drink
too little – or not at all – than to drink too much.

Some of the more popular drinks in the UK may be stronger in
alcohol than you think. Their alcohol by volume (ABV) content is
generally higher than some other drinks, such as traditional
bitters. A traditional bitter contains between 3 and 4% ABV, while
lagers such as *Stella Artois*, *Kronenbourg 1664,* and *Grolsch*
usually have around 5%. Wine has a higher alcohol content,
sometimes as high as 13 or 14 percent. (For the relationship
between ABV and units of alcohol, see the chart on page 13.)

Often we drink to have fun, to become more relaxed, or to
loosen up. Alcohol makes us feel less inhibited, even when we
aren't actually 'drunk.' While enjoying alcohol can be pleasant, if
we drink too much and it becomes addictive, the situations we'll
find ourselves in won't be so nice. That's why it's imperative that
we keep tabs on our alcohol consumption. Frequent and heavy
drinking not only damages the drinker's health and lifestyle, but it
also affects relationships with family, friends, and co-workers. If

Drinking alcohol affects blood
sugar levels and may make you
feel hungry

Alcohol is often used to
relax after a hard day, or
just to relax no matter
what type of day a person
has had. George Bernard
Shaw once said, 'Alcohol is
the anaesthesia by which
we endure the operation of
life.' Used wisely, alcoholic
beverages can take the
edge off an otherwise
stressful day. However,
used in excess, they can
cause even more problems
for the drinker.

Alcohol makes us feel less inhibited

the drinker realises his drinking is causing problems, and yet continues to drink, this may be an indication that he is addicted to alcohol and needs professional help to break the addiction.

Note that it's generally held to be a good idea not to drink at all during pregnancy. The risk of having a baby with FAS (foetal alcohol syndrome) is too great. The baby can be affected by problems with the central nervous system, facial abnormalities, and also a lower IQ. A woman who drinks while pregnant also risks having a low birth weight baby. It's best to avoid any consumption of alcohol until after the baby is born, and to consume very little (if any) as long as breast feeding continues.

If you believe you are drinking a bit too much – or a lot too much – begin keeping a journal to note how much your are drinking, when you are drinking, and with whom (see page 147). You can then assess whether or not you are consuming too much alcohol and decide what action you must take. It's possible there are situations you need to avoid – or people you need to avoid – at least until you get your drinking under control. Identifying the root of your alcohol problem, if there is one, is the first step to changing your drinking habits.

Tips to cut down on drinking
- Drink one non-alcoholic drink for every alcoholic drink you consume.
- Plan at least two days a week to abstain from alcohol.
- Drink slowly.
- Skip lunchtime drinks.
- Set a drinking limit before you go out.
- When you need to relax, opt for something besides alcohol, eg, a warm bath, soothing music, a book of poetry.

The adverse affects of alcohol have almost become common knowledge. However, despite that, heavy drinking among

Heavy drinking, in addition to the physical problems it causes, may also make the drinker look foolish or comical. According to Robert Benchley, 'Drinking makes such fools of people, and people are such fools to begin with, that it's compounding a felony.' When drinking at a party or gathering, make sure you don't end up the fool.

Photo: © iStockphoto.com, Mike Webber

The abuse of alcohol in public places is becoming more widespread

individuals of various ages and backgrounds remains prevalent and is actually increasing. Years ago, men were the heavy drinkers. However, these days, women and children are beginning to drink more. The fact that is disturbing – besides the prevalence of underage drinking – is that, despite the knowledge and information about alcohol dependency, people continue to imbibe. The main thing to remember is, if you're a heavy drinker, there is help. You only have to be willing to seek it out.

Ultimately, the motivation you need to make a change in your drinking habits may be close by. Think of the relationships you have with your significant other, your children, your co-workers, your friends. Are those relationships healthy? Or have they been adversely by your alcohol consumption? What about your finances? Your career? Has it suffered because of your drinking?

After you have read this manual, think about those questions. Answer them honestly. If you find your drinking does not affect those areas of your life and that you are consuming alcohol moderately . . . great! However, if you suspect you may have a problem with your drinking, re-read this manual, and seek help if necessary.

A word about units (and units)

This book has been written primarily for the UK market. The units of measurement therefore reflect the uniquely confused relationship which we have with the metric and Imperial systems (wine by the litre, beer by the pint; distance by miles, fuel by litres; timber cross-section in metric, length in Imperial, etc). The strength of alcoholic drinks is expressed as percentage alcohol by volume (% ABV) rather than by the now obsolete 'degrees proof'.

As far as units of alcohol are concerned, the UK standard has been adopted (1 unit = 10 ml pure alcohol). It is however interesting to note that although the recommended consumption limits in units of alcohol are similar worldwide, the sizes of the units are not. The UK has the smallest units in the world at 10 ml, whilst the largest are found in Japan at 25 ml.

9

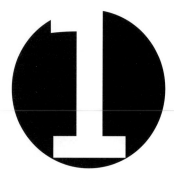

Alcohol and its effects

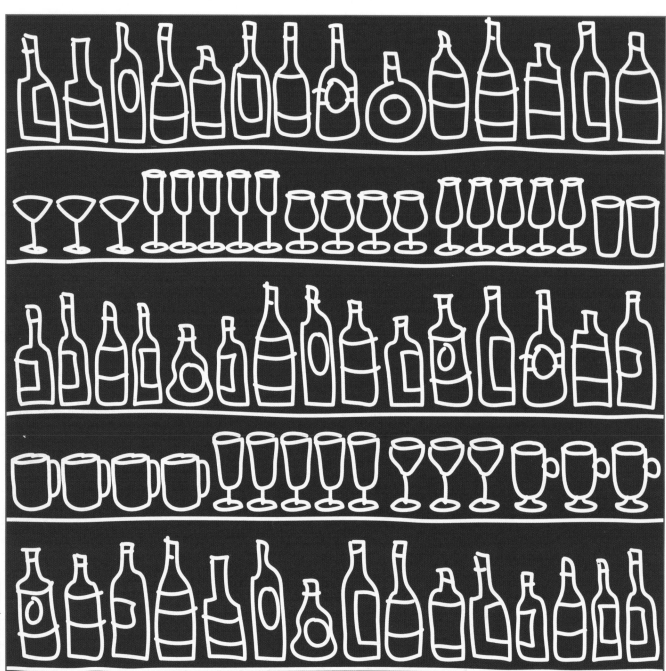

PART 1

Introduction

The word 'alcohol' is derived from the Arabic word 'al-ghawl' which means 'essence'. Alcohol may very well be the world's oldest known drug. Throughout history, it has been used in religious ceremonies, in medical treatments and for recreational purposes.

Just what is this mysterious substance? Alcohol is made by the fermentation of grain, potatoes, fruit juices, honey or sugar. The process of metabolizing carbohydrates by certain micro-organisms – otherwise known as yeasts – in the absence of oxygen creates alcohol. Distillation of fermented fruit or grain mixtures results in spirits such as whisky, rum, vodka, and gin. (In case you're wondering . . . Chemical modification of fossil fuels such as oil, natural gas, or coal results in industrial alcohol – not something you'd want to drink!)

To get a good understanding of the effects of alcohol, let's first take a look at the nature of alcohol as a chemical.

- Alcohol is made up of carbon, hydrogen and oxygen. Its chemical formula is C_2H_5OH.
- Alcohol is a clear liquid at room temperature.
- Alcohol will evaporate at a lower temperature than water.
- Alcohol mixes easily with water.
- Alcohol is flammable.

Today, the alcohol business is booming! Sadly, the problems linked to alcohol abuse have increased as well.

The chemical symbol for an ethanol molecule

Photo: © iStockphoto.com, Robert Kyllo

PART 1 Physical effects

Your body is like a finely-tuned engine. To keep your vehicle in good running order, you need to know how fuel affects your car. To keep your body functioning well, you need to know how substances affect it and which ones can cause a glitch in your system.

It is imperative that you know how to use alcohol safely– to have a great time without causing harm to yourself or others. No one intends to lose his licence, his life, or the lives of others. Finding out the effects of alcohol will go a long way in preventing harm coming your way.

There are several factors to consider when determining how alcohol affects us:
- Age.
- Gender.
- Physical condition/weight.
- Amount of food consumed.
- Other drugs/medications taken.
- Health problems, e.g. Gilbert's Syndrome.
- Other drugs/medications taken.

Knowing the strength of the alcohol you drink will help in making good choices. Drinks do not consist of pure alcohol; drinking only a few ounces of pure alcohol would quickly raise your blood alcohol level into the danger zone, which can be deadly.

The system used throughout Europe for measuring alcoholic strength is known as alcohol by volume (ABV), which expresses alcohol content as a percentage of the total volume of the drink. So a litre of wine at 12% ABV contains 120 ml (0.12 litre) of alcohol. The system used in the US and certain other countries expresses alcohol content as a percentage (or 'degrees') in comparison with a notional substance known as 'proof liquor'. US proof liquor is defined as 50% ABV, so 100 proof liquor is 50% ABV, 40 proof is 20% ABV, and so on.

On a positive note . . . Recent studies have shown that moderate – the key word is *moderate* – use of alcohol may have a **beneficial effect** on the coronary system. In general, for healthy individuals, one unit per day for women and no more than two units per day for men would be considered moderate use. (The use of the word 'healthy' refers to non-pregnant women, individuals not addicted to alcohol, and those without pre-existing medical conditions.)

There are several physical effects that alcohol has on the body. Primarily, it acts on the nerve cells within the brain, interfering with communication between the nerve cells and all other cells in the body.

You need to know how food and drink affects your body

H46076

The strength of alcoholic drinks
Typical alcohol concentrations by volume (ABV)

Beer = 4 to 6 %
Alcopops = 6 to 9 %
Wine = 9 to 15 %
Distilled spirits (vodka, whisky, gin etc) =
    37.5 to 40 % (a few are 50% or higher)

Just what is a 'drink' and what is a 'unit'?

Generally, a drink is considered in these amounts. Home measures tend to be larger:

- 125 ml (small glass) of wine
- 250 ml (large glass) of wine cooler/spritzer or alcopop
- Half a pint (284 ml) of beer
- 25 – 35 ml (single measure) of spirits

How do you calculate the amount of alcohol in your drink?

In the UK, one unit of alcohol is defined as 10 ml. So:

$$\frac{\text{ABV} \times \text{volume (ml)}}{1000} = \text{number of units}$$

ABV is the alcoholic strength of the drink as stated on the bottle.

For example: If you have a pint of lager at 5% ABV:

1 pint = 568 ml

$$\frac{5 \times 568}{1000} = 2.84, \text{ i.e. nearly 3 units.}$$

The alcoholic strength of spirits was originally tested by trying to set fire to gunpowder mixed with the spirit. If the mixture burned, the spirit was 100 proof or better. If it wouldn't burn, the spirit was 'under proof'.

Units of alcohol and ABV

If you know the strength of your drink in percentage alcohol by volume (ABV) and the size of the drink in millilitres (ml), you can work out the number of units of alcohol it contains from this chart. (1 unit = 10 ml of pure alcohol)

	Beers			Wines			Spirits		
	3%	4%	5%	10%	12%	14%	37.5%	40%	45%
25 ml	-	-	-	-	-	-	0.9	1.0	1.1
35 ml	-	-	-	-	-	-	1.3	1.4	1.6
50 ml	-	-	-	-	-	-	1.9	2.0	2.3
70 ml	-	-	-	-	-	-	2.6	2.8	3.2
125 ml	-	-	-	1.3	1.5	1.8	-	-	-
175 ml	-	-	-	1.8	2.1	2.5	-	-	-
250 ml	0.8	1.0	1.3	2.5	3.0	3.5	-	-	-
284 ml (½ pint)	0.9	1.1	1.4	-	-	-	-	-	-
568 ml (1 pint)	1.7	2.3	2.8	-	-	-	-	-	-
700 ml	2.1	2.8	3.5	7.0	8.4	9.8	26.3	28.0	31.5
750 ml	2.3	3.0	3.8	7.5	9.0	10.5	28.1	30.0	33.8
1000 ml	3.0	4.0	5.0	10.0	12.0	14.0	37.5	40.0	45.0

25 ml = 1 'old' single measure of spirits
35 ml = 1 'new' single measure of spirits
50 ml = 1 'old' double measure of spirits
70 ml = 1 'new' double measure of spirits
125 ml = 'small' wine glass
175 ml = 'medium' wine glass
250 ml = 'large' wine glass, European standard beer glass
700, 750 and 1000 ml = standard bottle sizes

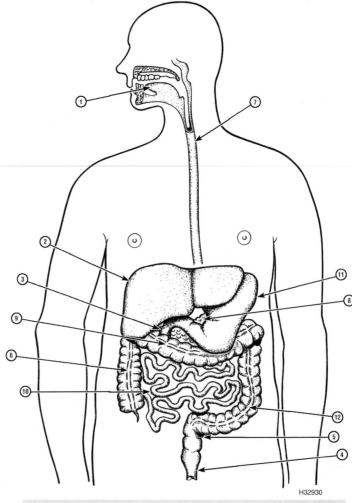

The digestive system

1 Tongue

2 Liver

3 Duodenum

4 Rectum

5 Caecum

6 Ascending colon

7 Oesophagus

8 Pancreas

9 Transverse colon

10 Small intestine

11 Stomach

12 Descending colon

H32930

The travels of *Jack Daniel's*

Jack Daniel's starts out in a bottle you find in your supermarket. Not content to sit on the shelf all his days, he appeals to you. Taking pity on the old boy, you purchase the bottle and free him from his sedentary life. Note the path your alcohol of choice takes:

1 It enters the body through the mouth.
2 Following the pathway into the stomach, some alcohol is absorbed into the bloodstream through the stomach lining; however, most of it travels on.
3 The remainder – and majority – of the alcohol that is absorbed enters the bloodstream through the walls of the small intestine.
4 The heart pumps the alcohol in the bloodstream throughout the body.
5 Alcohol reaches the brain.
6 Alcohol reaches the liver and is converted into water, carbon dioxide and energy at a rate of about 10 ml per hour.

Alcohol can be a 'downer' in that it reduces activity in the central nervous system. A drunken person will have lost muscle tone, a staggering gait, and often a loss of fine motor co-ordination.

The drunken person's eyes will appear glassy and his pupils may be slow to respond to stimulation/stimulus such as light.

In large quantities, alcohol can decrease your heart rate and lower your blood pressure/respiration rate. This can result in slower reflexes and reaction times, giving way to clumsiness.

Often a drunken person sweats profusely. His skin may feel both warm and clammy to the touch.

What does the world see in a drunken person?

A staggering, sweaty, smelly person who speaks too loudly, slurs his words, and is incredibly obnoxious. Oh, and he also thinks he is unbelievably funny – but he's the only one who thinks he is!

Typical effects of different levels of blood alcohol concentration (BAC)

Euphoria (BAC 0.03 – 0.12%)
- A relaxing effect (nice!).
- Reduction of tension.
- Lowering of inhibitions.
- Impaired concentration.
- Poor judgement.
- Legal limit for driving in UK is 0.08% (0.05% in most of Europe).

Confusion (BAC 0.10 – 0.25%)
- Slowed reflexes.
- Impaired reaction time.
- Reduced co-ordination.
- Drowsiness.
- Slurred speech.
- Altered emotions (What? Who says I'm angry? I'm not angry!).
- Vomiting.

Stupor (BAC 0.25 – 0.40%
- Breathing difficulties.
- Unconsciousness.
- Risk of death through inhaling vomit

Coma (BAC 0.35% or more)
- Coma.
- Death (this is getting serious!).

PART

Are you at risk?

People are different. We are different ages, sizes, genders, we take different medication, etc. Therefore, there are a number of factors that affect the way you will respond to alcohol.

- **Body weight** – A smaller person will reach a given Blood Alcohol Concentration (BAC) faster than a larger person.
- **Food consumption** – Food in the stomach slows down the absorption of alcohol; eating a substantial meal can slow it down by as much as 50%.
- **Drinking speed** – This affects the amount of alcohol in the bloodstream before being metabolised by the liver.
- **Environment** – Drinking at home may produce a different reaction to drinking in the pub or a more hostile environment.
- **History of drinking** – Previous experiences with alcohol may dictate your individual tolerance level and how much is needed to gain the same effects.
- **Expectations** – Often smaller quantities can create a desired effect if we have anticipated 'having a good time'.
- **Physical and mental health** – You can get drunk quickly if you have been ill, are tired, or are mentally or physically feeling down.
- **Gender** – Females, having less body fluid and more body fat, will have a higher BAC when drinking the same quantities as a man, even if they weigh the same. Menstruation and contraceptive pills can affect their reaction to alcohol, as can some prescription and recreational drugs. You should always be aware of this when drinking.

Units of alcohol and BAC

These charts show the **typical** blood alcohol concentration which can be expected after drinking a certain number of units. Note though that individuals vary widely in the rate at which they absorb alcohol. *There is no safe number of units which can be consumed before driving.*

Yellow	*driving noticeably impaired*
Orange	*in excess of permitted BAC for driving in UK*
Red	*danger of stupor, coma or death*

Men

No of units	Weight in stone (kg)						
	7 (44)	8 (51)	9 (57)	10 (64)	11 (70)	13 (83)	16 (102)
0	0	0	0	0	0	0	0
1	0.03	0.02	0.02	0.01	0.01	0.01	0.01
2	0.05	0.05	0.04	0.04	0.03	0.03	0.02
3	0.08	0.07	0.06	0.05	0.05	0.04	0.03
4	0.11	0.10	0.09	0.08	0.07	0.06	0.05
5	0.14	0.13	0.12	0.11	0.10	0.08	0.07
6	0.16	0.16	0.14	0.13	0.11	0.10	0.08
7	0.19	0.18	0.16	0.14	0.12	0.11	0.09
8	0.22	0.21	0.18	0.17	0.14	0.13	0.10
9	0.24	0.23	0.20	0.18	0.15	0.14	0.11
10	0.26	0.24	0.22	0.19	0.16	0.15	0.12

Women

No of units	Weight in stone (kg)						
	6½ (41)	7 (44)	8 (51)	9 (57)	10 (64)	11 (70)	13 (83)
0	0	0	0	0	0	0	0
1	0.04	0.04	0.03	0.03	0.03	0.02	0.02
2	0.07	0.07	0.06	0.06	0.05	0.04	0.04
3	0.10	0.09	0.08	0.08	0.07	0.06	0.06
4	0.15	0.14	0.13	0.11	0.10	0.09	0.08
5	0.19	0.18	0.16	0.14	0.12	0.11	0.10
6	0.22	0.22	0.19	0.17	0.14	0.13	0.12
7	0.25	0.23	0.21	0.19	0.16	0.15	0.14
8	0.29	0.27	0.24	0.22	0.19	0.17	0.16
9	0.32	0.30	0.27	0.25	0.21	0.19	0.17
10	0.35	0.32	0.30	0.27	0.23	0.20	0.18

Your finely-tuned engine

For most of us, when affected by alcohol, we assume it is acting on our brains. However, alcohol affects much more of our body than that. As you've read, once absorbed into the body, alcohol is distributed by our bloodstream to every part of our bodies. Because alcohol mixes with in water, it is found in body tissues, fluids and anywhere water is contained in the body. Given enough time, all of your blood will have the same amount of alcohol in it, whether it's streaming through your head or your feet!

Time to leave

Once alcohol has had its fun, it's time to leave. Alcohol leaves the body in three ways:

- Via the kidneys which eliminate 5% in the urine.
- Via the lungs where we exhale another 5%.
- Via the liver which chemically breaks down all the remaining alcohol into acetic acid, then into carbon dioxide, water and fats.

Although the liver cleanses the body of alcohol, it is a very slow process. It is eliminated through the body at approximately one unit (10 ml) of alcohol per hour. Therefore, one pint of 4% ABV lager (2.3 units) will take more than two hours to pass through your body. If you have had a lot to drink the evening before, you may find you are still over the limit the next day!

Statistics on alcohol-related deaths

In England and Wales, the number of alcohol-related deaths rose in the 1980s and 1990s. They have continued to rise since the year 2000. In 2001, the number of alcohol-related deaths was 5,970; however, by 2003, it had risen to 6,580. In 2003, death rates per 100,000 people increased to 11.6 from 10.7 in 2001. Two-thirds of the total numbers of 2003 deaths were men, making alcohol-related deaths much more common for males than females.

Alcohol consumption and BAC

Are you at risk? The key to non-harmful alcohol consumption lies with your knowledge of how much alcohol you can consume safely. That's the first step toward responsible drinking.

The tables earlier gave details of the effects of different levels of Blood Alcohol Concentration (BAC). Whilst BAC is obviously related to the number and strength of drinks you consume in a given time, there is no hard and fast rule for relating one to the other. As already mentioned, factors such as sex, age, weight, stomach contents and drinking history all affect the rate at which alcohol is absorbed into the bloodstream. This is why it is impossible to say with certainty how many units of alcohol a person can consume and still be legally 'safe' to drive.

Alcohol-related deaths in England and Wales (age-standardised per 100 000)

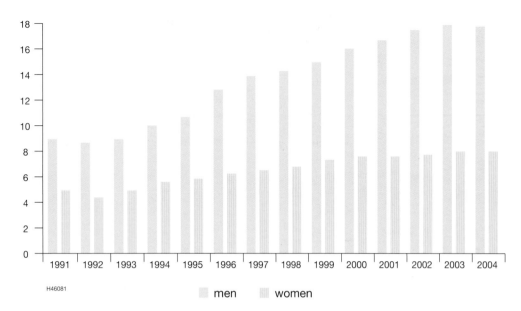

H46081

men   women

Alcohol-related deaths by region

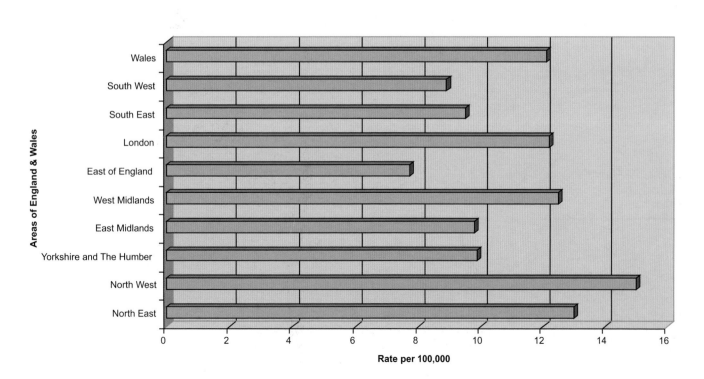

Alcohol-related deaths

Effects of alcoholism

Photo: © iStockphoto.com, Boris Zaytsev

How alcohol works on the body

People use alcohol to feel good, at least initially, and many believe society encourages drinking. Virtually all social events – and some business functions – offer alcoholic choices. As an addictive drug, over time alcohol can lead to cravings and impaired self-control. Even if the decision to drink is voluntary at first, what happens after a person takes a drink depends largely on his vulnerability to alcoholism and how his body and mind react to alcohol.

> "Alcoholism is a chronic disease with many similarities to asthma, diabetes, and high blood pressure."
> This provocative statement has been the cause of much debate.

A chronic disease is one that continues over a long period of time and progresses consistently as well as intermittently but that can be managed. The causes of chronic diseases are complex and often include hereditary factors. A chronic disease does not always follow a predictable course. Some patients tend to relapse more frequently than others, requiring a change of behaviour from the patient.

Alcoholism, asthma, diabetes and high blood pressure exhibit the following:
- Strong behavioural components.
- Strong genetic components.
- Identifiable by good diagnostic methods.
- Similar patterns of symptom control and relapse.

There are a number of very good reasons for treating alcohol as a chronic disease; these are taken from a great deal of evidence:

- Alcohol is a drug that affects people differently.
- The direct effect of alcohol on brain chemistry.
- Genetics and behaviour increase the risk of developing alcoholism.
- Alcoholism treated as an acute illness will negatively influence perceptions about treatment.
- New medications can help reduce cravings.
- Stigmas have led to treatment within the healthcare system being less available than treatment for other diseases.

People who are aware they are at genetic risk for asthma, diabetes, and high blood pressure can control certain risk factors. Similarly, individuals with family histories of alcoholism can reduce their risk by choosing not to drink or strictly limiting the amount they drink. This may be easier said than done, however, particularly for young people who may lack the maturity to make responsible decisions concerning their health.

For most of us – including health professionals – alcohol abuse is more often viewed as a social problem rather than a health issue. This appears to be related to the stigma and social disapproval that accompanies addictions of any kind. Therefore, often people do not get the treatment they need. Ultimately, this increases alcohol-related health care costs, reduces productivity in the workplace, and brings disruption to families.

New research indicates that there is a biological root to alcoholism and shows how changes in brain chemistry can lead to addiction. Medication has been developed to treat the problem. This means we can get prescribed medication in addition to behavioural therapy to manage alcoholism.

Alcohol's effect on unborn babies

Consumption of alcohol is the greatest cause of neurological damage to unborn children. When a mother drinks an excessive amount during pregnancy, Foetal Alcohol Syndrome can result. It is a pattern of mental and physical defects. It is generally agreed that alcohol in the mother's bloodstream enters the foetus by crossing the placenta. This interferes with the oxygen supply and nourishment necessary for normal cell development in the brain and other body organs.

Babies born with FAS often exhibit some if not all of the following symptoms:

- Short nose.
- Small eyes.
- Thinned upper lip.
- Small heads and brains.
- Poor co-ordination.
- Hyperactivity.

It is generally believed that for the avoidance of FAS, small amounts of alcohol on a regular basis are better than irregular drinking binges. However, to keep your unborn baby safe, it is advisable **not to drink at all.**

The brain game

Because alcohol is a very small molecule, it is soluble in lipid (fat) and water solutions. This makes it easily absorbable into the bloodstream and makes it easy to cross the BBB (Blood Brain Barrier). The BBB is semi-permeable. It allows some substances to cross through it but not all.

When someone drinks regularly and heavily, he or she is known as a *chronic* drinker. This affects their brain as well as their reactions. Often becoming addicted to alcohol, they find that if they try to kick the habit they experience undesirable consequences: they may shake (tremors) and/or suffer from insomnia. The more dependent a person is on alcohol, the more severe the symptoms.

Heavy drinking can:
- Affect the size of the brain.
- Create increased dependence on alcohol.
- Cause confusion and lack of memory.

Alcoholism is known to be a major health threat by many health professionals. Still, not enough is known about how alcoholism affects the brain. According to Enoch Gordis, Director of the US National Institute on Alcohol Abuse and Alcoholism, alcohol can have a specific set of effects on the brain and at the same time a number of effects that are very variable. For instance:

- Not everyone who has one drink has another.
- Most people who drink alcohol do not become addicted.
- Of those who do become addicted, some become violent, some become depressed.
- Many aspects vary widely.

Despite the different circumstances, all alcoholics show signs of regional brain damage and cognitive dysfunction. This is evident by using the latest technology of MRI scanning.

Alcohol and your body

Within minutes of alcohol entering your body, it infiltrates the bloodstream, the brain, liver, pancreas, kidneys, lungs, and every other organ and tissue system. The strength of the drink will have an impact on the absorption rate: the fastest absorption is of drinks in the range 10 – 20% ABV. Stronger and weaker drinks are absorbed more slowly.

Think about this
Alcohol in your body affects:
- Your liver.
- Your gastrointestinal tract.
- Your blood.
- Your muscles.
- Your central nervous system.
- Your endocrine system.
in fact – every part of the body.

Photo: © iStockphoto.com

When neat spirits are consumed in concentrated amounts, they can irritate the stomach lining, causing a response which delays absorption of the alcohol (although it will still be absorbed eventually, so drinking higher alcohol content drinks is not a means of minimising the effects of alcohol). The temperature of the alcohol also affects its absorption. Warm alcohol is absorbed faster than cold.

Almost as soon as we have some alcohol, it seems to have an effect on our central nervous system. It begins by depressing the inhibitory centres of the brain. We feel more relaxed and confident. Often a feeling of being able to 'let loose' is experienced.

This lessening of inhibitions gives rise to a person talking more confidently, perhaps increasing their attractiveness to others. This can be a positive effect of alcohol, provided the consumption is limited. However, as tolerance increases, larger amounts of alcohol are required to achieve the same positive effects.

What we often see instead in an alcoholic's drinking, is that as soon as the euphoric feeling has worn off, negative rebound effects are experienced. These may include feelings of depression, guilt, and anxiety that had been suppressed by the alcohol.

Alcohol often brings about a feeling of being able to 'let loose'

Once the euphoria evaporates, negative effects are experienced

Photo: © iStockphoto.com, Chris Schmidt

Tolerance: why can I drink and he can't?

Have you ever noticed how some people can drink more than others and how others simply cannot 'hold their liquor'? The key word is *tolerance.* People are different and have different tolerance levels.

As previously stated, alcohol is a drug. As such, when inside the body, it is able to produce these important effects:

Toxicity

All drugs, by their own chemical nature, are able to produce lesions – or physical damage – in the body. These lesions will be of a higher or lesser degree according to the time for which the person has been consuming and the quantity. This toxic effect takes place in various parts of the body. Much of it depends on the type of substance consumed and the characteristics of the consumer.

Addiction (dependence)

This is the effect that appears when a person makes excessive or abusive use of a substance during a certain time frame. Little by little, this generates a necessity to continue to consume until dependency takes hold and the person virtually loses their freedom of choice. At this point, the person becomes enslaved by his addiction, experiencing withdrawal symptoms both physically and psychologically.

Withdrawal Syndrome results when the person has no other solution than to consume alcohol (or other drugs) to maintain or re-establish a physical and emotional balance. It becomes a vicious cycle where it seems there is little choice than to continue to consume. Over time, both mental and physical health will deteriorate.

Tolerance

When a person is drinking or using a certain drug regularly, his body becomes accustomed to an abusive amount of the substance. The body, over a period of time, can require more of the substance to create the same effect.

Initial Tolerance: This refers to the small amount the body is capable of tolerating the first time we drink alcohol or take a drug. Each person is different and is born with a different 'initial tolerance'. Therefore, the quantity tolerated by one person may not be the same as that tolerated by another.

A person who abstains from consuming alcohol or makes moderate use of it will not experience a variation in tolerance during their lifetime. Whenever he takes in the same quantity, he will notice the same effects. This is a normal phenomenon that takes place.

However, when a person begins to accustom his body to a larger dose of alcohol regularly, the phenomenon of increasing tolerance occurs, consequently, the person needs to have a larger

quantity in order to get the same effect. This indicates that an addiction is being created.

Several situations can modify the tolerance. Initially, tolerance increases slowly as the person maintains an excessive consumption of alcohol over a significant period of time. If the person stops drinking, the tolerance level falls quickly until reaching its initial level, usually after several weeks. If drinking restarts, the tolerance returns to the same level that it was when last drinking.

Alcohol has a depressor effect on the brain

Sometimes the heavy drinker suddenly realises while still drinking – or rather, drinking the same amount as before – that he is no longer able to tolerate it. Tolerance rapidly declines. This is an indicator that the nervous system is seriously affected. Taking the example below, the outcome is that the spring collapses. There is not enough force to push it up to keep the balance.

The effect of drinking alcohol is like having a weight in the brain that forces it to work harder. Imagine a tray of drinks on top of a spring. When the alcohol begins to act, there will be a force down that the brain has to counteract by pushing upwards to maintain the same balance point. When the effects of the alcohol disappear, the spring shoots up because the brain has not had enough time to readjust. For that reason, it appears that the nervous system works faster. Ultimately, withdrawal symptoms will appear: hangover, tremor of hands, hot/cold sweats, etc.

Alcohol affects various parts of the brain. However, different parts are not equally affected. Some are more sensitive to the effects of alcohol than others. However, as the quantity of alcohol in the bloodstream increases, more and more parts of the brain are affected.

Alcohol affects the brain centres in a set order

1 Cerebral cortex
2 The limbic system
3 Cerebellum
4 Hypothalamus
5 Medulla (brain stem)

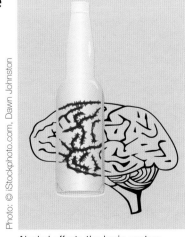

Photo: © iStockphoto.com, Dawn Johnston

Alcohol affects the brain centres

The cerebral cortex

This is the largest portion of the brain. It processes information such as thought and consciousness. In combination with an area called the basal ganglia, it controls most of the voluntary muscle movements we have as well as affecting the low order brain centres. Acting on the cortex, alcohol has the following effects:

- Make a person more lively/talkative and less inhibited.
- Thought processes are slowed; judgement becomes impaired.
- Senses (smelling, taste, touch, vision, hearing) are affected or 'blunted'.
- Threshold of pain is numbed.

As our blood alcohol level increases, these effects become more pronounced.

The limbic system

This is the hippocampus and septal area. It controls outer memory and emotions. When this part of our brain is affected by alcohol, our emotions are altered and memory loss may be evident to others.

The cerebellum

This area is where muscle movement is co-ordinated. If the cerebellum is not functioning properly, standing on one leg or touching your nose with your finger will become difficult or impossible. When affected by alcohol, our movements become jerky and uncontrolled. Because the cerebellum also controls our balance, we often find that drunken people fall over.

Hypothalamus and pituitary gland

This area of the brain co-ordinates chemical and endocrine functions (thyroid, growth and sex hormone secretion) via the pituitary gland as well as a number of automatic functions of the brain through the medulla. There are two noticeable effects alcohol has on this part of the brain:

- Increased urine excretion by inhibiting the secretion of a hormone that helps the kidneys re-absorb water.
- Sexual function is affected. Arousal is increased but performance is decreased.

Medulla

This part of the brain controls all of our involuntary bodily functions – those functions we generally don't think about – like heart rate, temperature, breathing, and consciousness. Under the influence of alcohol, a person may begin to feel sleepy and may eventually become unconscious. Should the blood alcohol content (BAC) keep increasing, breathing will slow and sometimes even stop. Blood pressure and body temperature will drop to dangerous levels.

Methyphobia (or Potophobia) is the fear of alcohol

Other effects of alcohol consumption
- Muscles experience reduced blood flow, causing us to feel aches and pains, particularly when recovering from a hangover.
- Blood flow increases to the stomach and intestines giving us an 'acid' tummy.
- Blood flow to the skin increases causing sweating; body heat is lost and body temperature may actually fall below normal.
- Irritation of the stomach lining which can lead to vomiting.

What's the big deal about blood alcohol levels?
As we've learned, alcohol affects individuals differently. Much depends on the amount of the alcohol consumed, the strength of the alcohol, and the tolerance level. Your blood alcohol level may also be affected by your age, gender, physical condition, amount of food consumed, and drugs/medication. It is always important to know how much and the concentration of alcohol you consume.

It's in the jeans . . . er, genes!
Research shows that genetic factors may contribute to the development of alcoholism, and that family is often the context for this to occur. There appears to be evidence that biological relatives are more likely to develop a problem with alcohol if there is a history of it in the family. The brother/sister and parent/child relationships increase the risk as well.

Adoption studies have been used to determine the validity of the genetic component of alcoholism. There is a very strong link, although there is an equally strong indicator that children learn through experience and observation. What we therefore find is that genetic, biological components and social interaction all play a part in creating an environment for creating alcoholic tendencies.

So . . . is alcoholism inherited?
There is some evidence that it could be, but science has yet to find a direct genetic link. Although researchers know that alcohol-use behaviour and disorders are significantly genetic in nature, identification of the specific genes that contribute to an individual's susceptibility for alcohol dependence has been difficult.

Many investigators have examined alcohol dependence in relation to its component parts (phenotypes) to better understand the genetic bases of alcohol use and dependence. It has been known for some time that the influence of a person's genes and the influence of their childhood environment (alcoholic/abusive parent), might conflict or conspire together to create a greater chance of them becoming addicted to alcohol or repeating a family pattern.

There is no major psychiatric disease that does not have genetic links. We are all predisposed to certain physical and mental illnesses. This means we are more likely to acquire the same diseases that visited the members of our families. Cancer and coronary artery diseases run in families; depression and anxiety run in families; and alcoholism runs in families.

According to one theory, cells are programmed at birth to react in certain ways when alcohol is in the body. Many children of alcoholics drink more before they feel intoxicating effects. They have a programmed need to drink more to get the same desired effect. Some people genetically predisposed to alcoholism metabolise alcohol differently. Many people who are chemically dependent were predisposed to the illness before they were born*.

* *Anthenelli and Schuckit 1994; Woodward 1994*

Percent in the UK consuming over the recommended weekly limits (21 units for men, 14 units for women)

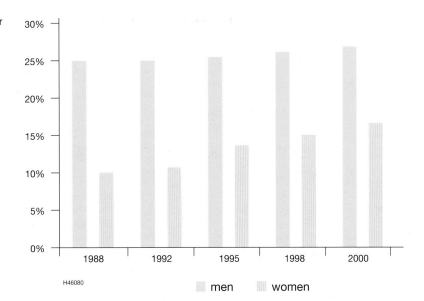

H46080

men   women

Percent in the UK consuming over the recommended daily limits (8 units for men, 6 units for women)

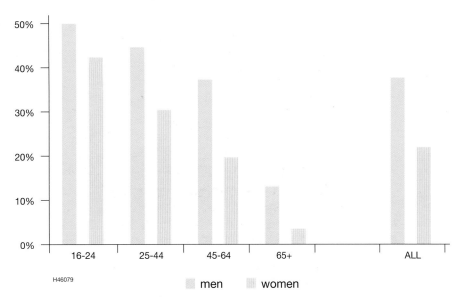

H46079

men   women

Percent of adults (by age and gender) in the UK consuming over double the recommended daily limits of alcohol

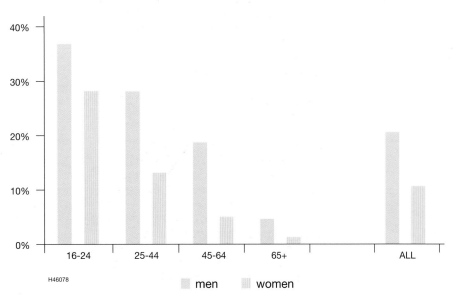

H46078

men   women

PART ② How alcohol affects nutrition

There are numerous theories as to the purpose of the indentation ("punt") at the bottom of a wine bottle:
- To strengthen the structure of the bottle.
- To collect sediment.
- To ensure stability.
- To make the bottle look bigger!
- No purpose, it was just how early glass-blowers turned them out.

Good nutrition is important to us as human beings. At the risk of stating the obvious, our bodies thrive on it! The main functions of nutrition are to provide energy and to maintain body function/structure. If we substitute alcohol for a well-balanced meal, we are doing a disservice to ourselves. Food supplies are like fuel for our finely tuned vehicle. Without fuel, a car won't run; without food, we can't function and will eventually die. Alcoholics tend to either replace meals with alcohol, or make poor nutritional choices in their food selection. This, in itself, is detrimental to health. However, to compound the problem, alcohol interferes with the digestion, storage, and utilisation of whatever nutrients we do consume. When alcohol replaces vital nutrients long-term, malnutrition disturbances will become evident.

H44846

Good nutrition is important to provide energy and maintain body function/structure

Moderation vs. Inebriation

When alcohol does not take the place of balanced meals, as in the moderate drinker, it may actually increase the appetite. However, alcoholics sometimes become malnourished because of the amount of alcohol they consume depressing their appetites. While alcohol may be rich in energy at seven calories per gram, it is devoid of any essential nutrients. The more alcohol consumed, the less likely an individual will eat enough nutrient-rich food to gain adequate nutrients. And even the energy we gain from the calories in alcohol is 'empty' – it has no nutritional value.

Lack of good food isn't the only thing that will cause malnutrition in an alcoholic. The drink itself, as mentioned above, interferes with digestion. The effect it has on the metabolism of nutrients can lead to liver damage, digestive system damage, and other organ damage.

Depending on a person's natural body type, malnutrition may not surface right away. In heavy drinkers, the following water-soluble vitamins are found to be deficient:

- Vitamin B6.
- Vitamin B12.
- Riboflavin.
- Thiamine.
- Vitamin C.
- Folic Acid.

And the following fat-soluble vitamins:
- Vitamin A.
- Vitamin E.
- Vitamin D.
- Vitamin K.

Alcohol intake also affects mineral absorption, including selenium, zinc, magnesium and iron.

Alcohol's effect on the gastrointestinal (GI) tract

The GI tract's purpose is to break down ingested food and provide absorption of nutrients, then to excrete the waste that's left over. Even in a healthy person, once alcohol is introduced, interesting things begin to happen. As the alcohol directly contacts the lining of the GI tract, it may lead to mucosal damage causing diarrhoea, or even bleeding within the tract. Once mucosal damage occurs, digestion is disturbed; nutrients aren't absorbed as efficiently into the body. Often this is evident in alcoholics as they frequently lose weight, while still maintaining what is known as a 'beer gut'. Not only does this damage prevent nutrients from being absorbed, it also increases the risk of toxins passing into the blood or lymph, causing damage not only to the liver but to other organs as well.

Alcohol makes the liver unable to absorb amino acids properly, hampering its effectiveness. It then cannot produce protein that is needed by the body to function properly. Also, alcohol increases the amount of fat in the blood. Fatty infiltration into the liver causes liver damage. The increased fat in the bloodstream is known as hyperlipidemia and can also be a risk factor for heart disease and high blood pressure.

Often, when alcohol consumption is high, food intake is reduced. This may be from 'forgetting' to eat due to a lack of appetite. Over a long period of time the body can become malnourished and depleted of essential vitamins and minerals.

Alcohol is linked to cancers of the mouth, throat, gullet and liver

H44837

This will not only result in reduced energy but can also cause mood swings and mild depression, and contribute to the onset of disease. There may also be an increase in the free radical activity in the body. Free radicals are 'scavengers' that will attach to cells and start to oxidise them, a process a bit like fruit rotting or a car rusting.

Alcohol has a high Glycaemic Index. In other words, it leaves too much sugar in the blood. That, in itself, can contribute to the onset of Type 2 diabetes. Changes in metabolism cause the body to become acidic making it difficult to lose weight and allowing disease to flourish.

Damage to the pancreas, stomach, oesophagus and the liver can occur as well as increased risk of cancer developing in the mouth or larynx.

As magnesium is depleted by high alcohol intake, the 'shakes' are a sure sign of magnesium deficiency.

Alcohol's effects on the mouth and the oesophagus

In the normal process of consuming alcohol, the mouth, oesophagus and stomach are exposed to it. Not surprisingly, mucosal lesions are found in people who are heavy drinkers. The tongue may be inflamed causing glossitis, while inflammation of the mouth is known as stomatitis. Many times an alcoholic will experience heartburn and GERD (GastroEsophageal Reflux Disease, commonly known as acid reflux). In some cases, the drinker will develop tooth decay, gum disease, and – as the disease advances – loss of teeth.

Metabolic consequences of drinking

Result of low protein levels

Weakness

Low albumin level

Poor healing capacity

Liver coma

Suggestions to counteract malnutrition

Replenish protein level with high quality and high quantity of protein

Limit protein and/or use of antibiotics

Eat a diet high in fruits and vegetables

Administer amino acids intravenously, if necessary (don't try this at home!)

Result of low carbohydrate levels

Diabetes

Wide fluctuations in blood sugar level

Limit intake of sugars

Eat regular, balanced meals and frequent snacks

Eat a diet high in protein and complex carbohydrates

Result of low fat levels

Hypertriglyceridemia

Hypercholesterolemia

Reduce intake of fat and sugars

Eliminate consumption of alcohol

Lower intake of fat and cholesterol

Result of low vitamin levels

Severe forgetfulness

Neuritis

Skin diseases

Poor healing ability

Susceptibility to infections

Take vitamin supplements until vitamin levels are replenished

Result of low mineral levels

Physical weakness

Heart irregularities

Anaemia

Muscle spasms

Eat regular, well-balanced meals

Take mineral supplements until normal levels are restored

Skin diseases

Source: Hauser, M, Iber, F. *Nutritional Advice and Diet Instruction in Alcoholism Treatment.* Alcohol Health & Research World. 1989; 13 (3): 261-266

Is there any good news?

Once the over-consumption ceases, the liver has an amazing ability to recuperate, provided it is not too damaged. There is also emerging evidence which suggests that coffee drinkers are at lower risk of liver damage due to alcohol, but this should not be used as an excuse for excessive consumption!

Taking steps to overcome months or even years of alcohol addiction is key. Eating a balanced diet is a good step. However, it may not be enough to supply the necessary nutrients for fighting the detrimental effects of prolonged alcohol abuse.

Vitamin and mineral supplements, along with antioxidants and amino acids, may be necessary. Those with health problems might want to discuss this with their pharmacist or GP / Primary Care Team.

You may want to try a gentle liver flush. Blend together 2 tablespoons olive oil, 4 tablespoons lemon juice, and a pinch of cayenne pepper. Drink immediately first thing in the morning and do not eat for an hour afterwards. Repeat this each day for one week.

Make sure to eat regular and well-balanced meals. Reducing sugar in your diet will help. Increasing your fruits and vegetables is imperative. Foods such as bananas, watermelon, oranges, figs, potatoes, tomatoes, and any type of greens have plenty of nutrients. Also, oats are excellent in fending off high cholesterol. Be sure you are drinking at least a litre and a half of water daily.

Guidelines to healthy nutrition
- Begin each day with breakfast.
- Do not rush through meals.
- Eat a variety of healthy foods.
- Take supplements if prescribed by your GP.
- Eat more fruit and less sweets.
- Do not allow yourself to get hungry – snack healthy!

Books to read
Note: *Foetal may be spelled fetal on many websites and book lists.*

Foetal Alcohol Syndrome: A Guide for Families and Communities. Ann Pytkowicz Streissguth (Brookes Publishing Company, 1997)

Message in a Bottle: The Making of Foetal Alcohol Syndrome. Janet Golden (Harvard University Press, 2005)

Foetal Alcohol Syndrome: From Mechanism to Prevention. E.L. Abel (CRC-Press, 1996)

Neuropharmacology of Ethanol. R.E. Meyer (Editor), G.F. Koob (Editor), M.J. Lewis (Editor), S.M. Paul (Editor) (Birkhauser, 1991)

Alcohol and the Addictive Brain: New Hope for Alcoholics from Biogenetic Research. Kenneth Blum, James E. Payne (Free Press, 1991)

Methods in Alcohol-related Neuroscience Research (Methods & New Frontiers in Neuroscience). Yuan Liu (Editor), David M. Lovinger (Editor) (CRC, 2002)

Health Issues Related to Alcohol Consumption. Ilsi Europe, Macdonald (Editor) (Blackwell Publishers, 1999)

The Genetics of Alcoholism (Alcohol & Alcoholism). Henri Begleiter (Editor), Benjamin Kissin (Editor) (Oxford University Press, US, 1995)

Toward a Molecular Basis of Alcohol Use and Abuse (Exs (Experientia Supplementum)). B. Jansson (Editor), H. Joernvall (Editor), U. Rydberg (Editor), L. Terenius (Editor), B.L. Vallee (Editor) (Birkhauser Boston, 1994)

Internet
www.well.com/user/woa/fsfas.htm

3 Psychological effects of alcohol

PART 3

Who ... me? Personality changes

Your psychological make-up is much of what makes you who you are. There are many influences that factor into a person's behaviour. Once alcohol is thrown into the mix, even more psychological changes occur.

When we begin to examine the psychological effects of alcohol, we need to be aware of the following and how they influence behaviour and reactions:

- Age.
- Economic status.
- Cultural aspects.
- Personal relationships.
- Personality.
- Job status.
- Physical effects of alcohol.
- Amount of alcohol consumed during a given time.

There are times when negative psychological effects occur. Often, they become a vicious cycle when a person drinks to block out the feelings or effects the alcohol has had upon them. The following are negative effects that may occur with heavy alcohol usage:

Depression

When a person is unable to concentrate, feels extremely sad, guilty, helpless, and hopeless, he is experiencing depression. He may also experience a loss of appetite and have thoughts of death. At times a person may turn to alcohol to block out feelings of depression. However, since alcohol actually inhibits the central nervous system, the opposite effect occurs. Sure, alcohol can provide a 'feel good' factor. But, after a time, more and more is needed to reach that 'high'. A large number of suicides and attempted suicides are related to alcohol abuse. Alcohol may also cause depression if it is the culprit in losing one's family, job, etc.

Poor self-image

When people have a poor self-image, they lack confidence. Often they turn to alcohol for a boost in confidence. However, this 'pseudo-confidence' is short-lived and will require larger and larger quantities to keep the good feeling going. Even those who have a reasonably good self-confidence often lose self-respect as their drinking increases, experiencing feelings of guilt.

Guilt

Self-reproach, whether real or imagined, is a negative feeling of inadequacy. It often shows up as a result of alcohol addiction. However, alcohol may be used to blot out guilty feelings related to other areas of the person's life.

Anxiety

Uncertainty and fear, whether due to a real or imagined threat, can cause symptoms of uneasiness, sweating, increased heart rate, or insomnia. These signs of anxiety are often found in people who drink and in those who experience withdrawal symptoms when they try to quit. Alcohol has been proven to increase anxiety, as the drinking itself can lead to anxiety-provoking situations.

Paranoid attitude

Suspicion of others is a state that is often compounded by the use of alcohol. It can be seen in the alcoholic while he is drinking as well as when he is experiencing withdrawal symptoms such as Delirium Tremens. Sometimes the alcoholic is worried about others whom they feel are aware of their drinking problem.

Extreme jealousy

Unwarranted jealousy is often found in close relationships where one or both partners are dependent on alcohol. Often this problem is compounded by the fact that one partner might find the drinking partner increasingly unattractive as he drinks to excess.

Denial

This is one of the most common reactions of an alcoholic. At times, it can be attributed to social reinforcement of drinking or a fear of being stigmatised. It can also be the result of fear of losing a job, breakdown of a marriage, or the inability to face up to a problem created by the individual's alcoholism.

Emotional disturbance

Commonly, people who drink too much become emotionally disturbed with extremes of emotion taking place. For example:

Violence

- Violence can lead to a breakdown in relationships, to prison sentences – in severe cases – and, generally, to a breakdown in normal life for the drinker.

Aggression

- Aggression can affect the person's response at work, their interaction with others and a general deterioration in lifestyle.

Anxiety/agitation

- Anxiety and agitation can cause unhappiness to the person as they find themselves increasingly unable to function normally, unable to socialise, and unable to complete mundane tasks. All this can lead to feelings of social inadequacy.

Social inadequacy

This can often affect those who have been raised in insecure environments, particularly if they have experienced parental disharmony. Social inadequacy can also be a result of addictive behaviour where a loss of coping mechanisms creates a use for alcohol as a substitute. Social skills may not only be affected but eroded.

The drinker may become socially isolated

Social withdrawal

The alcoholic may find it difficult to cope with life and its tasks on a daily basis. Eventually, as other psychological factors are adversely affected, the drinker may become increasingly isolated. It's easier to hide his problem if he withdraws from friends, family, etc.

Manipulation

Often the drinker blames others and using them as an excuse for continuing to drink excessively. Sometimes the manipulation is more subtle, like suggesting an outing that will involve alcohol. This is a ploy to avoid responsibility for their own problem and putting the blame on others, thereby creating a situation in which the drinker appears to be the 'victim'.

Phobic states

Similar to anxiety, this begins as anxiety yet escalates into a full-fledged phobia. It is more commonly found in people who drink in isolation and have already withdrawn from society.

PART

Is alcohol *really* that addictive?

A significant factor in determining how deeply one can be consumed in addiction is the state of a person's mental health prior to their addiction. Because we are all different, not everyone who becomes an alcoholic will have the same experiences. However, there are a number of common psychological symptoms that most addicts experience at some stage. These symptoms may become severe because of the way the addiction impacts the person's life.

A person is more likely to suffer psychologically if they are going through difficult times such as being unemployed, homeless, or physically unwell. With an alcohol addiction, long-term psychological harm may result due to brain damage and often once brain damage occurs, it is irreparable.

It is vital to remember that people can die from alcohol addiction. Death can come slowly due to a debilitating disease, such as cirrhosis, or it may come quickly via a heart attack. Alcoholism should definitely be taken seriously.

They psychological effects of addiction can be divided into those that relate to *feeling* and those that relate to *thinking*. Thoughts and feelings may lead to isolation if the drinker avoids others because of his addiction, feelings of inadequacy, and feelings of guilt. Then the drinker will compensate by drinking more heavily to avoid the bad feelings, which produces more of the same bad feelings. A vicious cycle ensues.

'I'm only hurting myself'

Contrary to what the alcoholic may think, his addiction is not only hurting himself, but those who love and care for him as well as casual acquaintances. Even so, family members tend to experience the greatest distress.

Feelings

The feeling of being unable to gain control of themselves concerning their drinking is common among alcoholics. They will find themselves behaving in ways which are not normal for him. Guilt and shame will ensue. When sober, the reality of this behaviour will hit home. This is when the guilt and shame will flood over the drinker.

Other feelings come from the drinker finding himself in a mess he is unable to cope with. It seems every decision he makes is a bad decision. Or, worse yet, he withdraws, accepts little or no responsibility and makes no decisions concerning his life at all.

In the beginning, he probably saw alcohol as a way to alter his mood, making him feel better, happier, the life and soul of the party. However, once addicted, he realises – too late – this euphoria is short-lived. Looking at the long-term effects of his drinking will show that the exact opposite has occurred. Inevitably, he will experience not only the negative effects listed previously, but also anger in varying degrees. He may begin experiencing grumpiness, which escalates to irritability, which rockets to explosive anger. Boredom may set in as the pattern of the addiction repeats so often it becomes boring in itself. Soon, the alcoholic has no confidence left and is seen to be anxious, depressed, and generally out of sorts.

Thinking

When a person drinks regularly he reaches the point where his is a habitual drinker. At this point, his thought patterns become defensive and he works to protect the addiction. This includes:

Dependency
• Believing others are responsible and can fix him.

Denying reality
• Convincing himself and those around him that his problem is not all that bad.

Grandiosity
• Thinking his own concerns are more important than anything else, as in, an 'It's all about ME' attitude.

Obsessive
• He focuses solely on the alcohol and plans his next drink before finishing his last one.

Self harm
• In desperation, the alcoholic thinks about harming himself to alleviate some of the mental and physical pain he is experiencing.

'If only . . .'
• Wishful thinking on the alcoholics part as he focusing on anything other than the real thing that needs changing – his addiction.

Mental ability
• The alcoholic's memory and concentration are adversely impaired.

Behaviour

How an alcoholic behaves is very much a reflection of his consuming relationship with alcohol. He may postpone changing his behaviour and having to face reality. Often his behaviour is a way of avoiding the extreme discomfort of withdrawal. Typical behaviours may include:

Self harm
• As mentioned above; he may also use this as a way to punish himself or to create a feeling of relief.

Betrayal
• People and good intentions are sacrificed as the almighty alcohol comes first in his life.

Avoiding
• The alcoholic chooses not to take responsibility for his life and becomes isolated.

Controlling
• He manipulates both people and circumstances for the sake of alcohol, sometimes resorting to violence.

Deception
• He deceives himself and others to avoid facing the consequences.

Don't worry – be happy!

PART **3**

Drinking alcohol is the leading cause of dancing like an idiot.

There are positive affects to alcohol that will be given in greater depth in a later chapter, *Having fun with alcohol*. It is imperative to remember that many things are good in moderation but are deadly if taken to the extreme. Alcohol consumption is like that. The key word is *moderation*.

In order to drink successfully, one must exercise restraint and discipline. If you find you cannot stop after a drink or two, you may need to abstain altogether. If, on the other hand, you can control the amount you drink, you may find that drinking in moderation is beneficial to you.

Some of the positive effects of alcohol consumption are the ease in which you can get livelier and relaxed. Drinking alcohol loosens up inhibitions, giving the feeling of euphoria. Socially, moderate consumption of alcohol may enable you to 'have a good time' while interacting with others.

Most important is to monitor your alcohol consumption. If you suspect you are drinking more than you should, it's time to cut back. Knowing when to slow your consumption or stop altogether is key to responsible drinking. When you can do that, you will find you can enjoy alcohol and its effects.

Sign that you drink too much

You have a bruise on the back of your head that, interestingly, matches the contours of your toilet seat.

Photo: © iStockphoto.com, Simon Moran

PART 3 **The downside**

Excessive consumption of alcohol may cause undue distress for the drinker and those around him. It can also lead the heavy drinker through the following – not necessarily pleasurable – stages.

Drinking alcohol may make you forget your ex-girlfriend won't appreciate a call from you at 2 in the morning.

While you were drinking . . .

Stage 1 – Clever

* This is when you suddenly become an expert on every subject in the known universe. You know you know everything and you want to pass on your knowledge to anyone who will listen. At this stage, you are *always* right. And, of course, the person you are talking to is very wrong. This makes for an interesting argument when both parties are *clever*.

Stage 2 – Attractive

* This is when you realise that you are the most *attractive* person in the entire bar and that everyone fancies you. You can go up to a perfect stranger knowing that they fancy you and really want to talk to you. Bear in mind that you are still *clever*, so you can talk to this person about anything under the sun.

Stage 3 – Rich

* This is when you suddenly become the richest person in the room. You can buy drinks for the entire bar because you have a bottomless wallet. You can also make bets at this stage because, of course, you are still *clever*, so naturally, you will always win. Anyway, it doesn't matter how much you bet, because you are *rich*. You will also buy drinks for everyone you fancy, in the knowledge that you are clearly the most *attractive* person present.

Stage 4 – Invincible

* You are now ready to pick fights with anyone and everyone, especially those with whom you have been betting or arguing. This is because you are now *invincible*. At this point, you can also go up to the partners of the people whom you fancy and challenge them to a battle of wits or strength. You have no fear of losing this battle because, as well as being *invincible*, you are *clever*, you're *rich*, and you're more *attractive* than them anyway.

Stage 5 – Invisible

* This is the final stage of drunkenness. At this point you can do anything, because you are now *invisible*. You can dance on a table to impress people who you fancy because the rest of the people in the room cannot see you. You can also snog the face off them for the same reason. You are also *invisible* to the people who want to fight you. You can walk through the street singing at the top of your lungs because no one can see or hear you and because you're still *clever*, you know all the words.

Suddenly you're an expert . . .

H46073

. . . and the richest person in the world

Time to get sober . . .

Stage 1 – Stupid
- As you regain consciousness and begin to enjoy the headache, the churning stomach, and the cold sweats, you realise that you have lost not only several hours of your life, but also the ability to concentrate on anything whatsoever. You are now *stupid* and will remain so for a minimum of 12 hours.

Stage 2 – Ugly
- Never entirely happy with the effects of the bathroom mirror first thing, you are horrified to discover that you have now become even *uglier* than you previously thought possible. Not only have you bloodshot eyes and a glorious collection of spots but you are shaking so much that your grandfather probably looks healthier. Unfortunately, you are still too *stupid* to know better than to try and shave whilst shaking.

Stage 3 – Poor
- Having crawled out of bed and got dressed, you are about to shamble out the door when you discover that the money that was to last you the week is missing from your wallet. Being *stupid*, you have no idea what happened to it but the traces of curry on your clothes allow the possibility that you might have treated everyone to a takeaway at some point. Alternately, your pocket could have been picked or you might have given the taxi driver a fifty by mistake. Rationalising that you couldn't possibly have been that *stupid* and that you would remember being robbed, you come to believe that you were the only one who bought any food or drinks all night and start to loathe all your friends.

Stage 4 – Fragile
- As you are now *stupid*, *ugly*, and *poor*, your consequently *fragile* self-esteem now plummets. Your already *fragile* physical condition ensures that you feel liable to shatter if anyone even speaks to you.

Stage 5 – Conspicuous
- This is the final stage of sobering up. Unfortunately, everyone can spot this *conspicuous* condition and its cause from a great distance. Even worse, they know that they can complete your misery by making fun of you, and that you are too *stupid* to retaliate, too *fragile* to hit them, too *poor* to bribe them, and too *ugly* to hide.

Psychological and physical diseases
Some of the psychological and physical diseases that may occur due to alcoholism are:

Delirium tremens
- *What's that I see?* Delirium tremens, commonly known as DTs, are episodes of hallucinations that may occur during withdrawal from alcoholism. It is usually preceded by loss of sleep and irritability, and develops after the alcoholic has gone without alcohol for a few days. In severe cases it may lead to heart attack or death. However, a GP can prescribe treatment to alleviate the symptoms of withdrawal.

Wernicke-Korsakoff Syndrome
- Alcoholism can cause a thiamine deficiency that leads to Wernicke-Korsakoff Syndrome. (Wernicke's encephalopathy and Korsakoff's psychosis). It generally occurs in alcoholics who fail to eat nutrient-rich foods. Signs are hard to distinguish from drunkenness – agitation, confusion, etc, – except that they continue to present themselves. Treatment includes a regimen of B vitamins (typically Thiamine and Vitamin B Compound Strong).

Depression
- The problem with depression is sometimes it seems to never go away. Major episodes may last one or more years if not treated. It not only affects a person's attitudes, thoughts, and perceptions, but it affects his physical well being also. Major depression may cause a person to move slowly and feel heaviness in the arms and legs; the victim may neglect his personal hygiene and stay in bed most of the time. In deep depression, suicidal thoughts frequently occupy the mind. Without treatment, the severely depressed alcoholic may attempt suicide.

H32859

Which is the way out?

While psychological problems can result from drinking too much, many can be overcome when the alcoholic chooses to say 'no' to the drink. If your drinking has progressed into alcoholism, you may need to abstain completely. Moderate drinking may not be a viable option once an addiction has been formed. However, for those who have never experienced the addictive effects of alcohol, drinking in moderation should not cause any psychological problems to develop.

Alcohol and work

Photo: © iStockphoto.com, Simone van den Berg

PART 4 Work

A vocation can help you have a purpose and focus in life. It can give you reasons to help others and leave something for future generations to enjoy, such as art or literature. Or your vocational choice can give others something to build on, such as an education, a business, or a charitable organisation.

Most importantly, there should be a good balance with any alcohol consumption and our home and work life. If not, problems can occur. If the balance is right, we should be able to drink alcohol responsibly while maintaining a successful career. The significant thing is to remember – above all – to drink only in moderation.

Sometimes colleagues meet up for a quick one (or two) after work

The workplace

The work environment can have an effect on a person's drinking. The employee's senior management team, as well as his work mates, can often set the tone of the drinking culture in a company. If they encourage drinking by condoning alcoholic lunches and time off to play then this can be viewed by other employees as an encouragement to increase their drinking. Sometimes, because of seniority, managers will have more time to drink and be able to attend long lunches or business functions where alcohol is served.

There are many factors in the workplace that can make a person more vulnerable to drinking. If an employee's work is made up of repetitive tasks, boredom may set in, and an increase in alcohol consumption may occur. Also a general lack of control over work, including demanding tasks and irrational deadlines set by management are other factors. If harassment occurs in the workplace – be it sexual or verbal – it can affect an employee to the point where he may turn to drinking as a way of escape.

For many people, working away from home for extended periods of time or being 'on the road' can also lead to increased alcohol consumption. Often when in a strange location, drinking is viewed as a sociable way of fitting in. For a person who travels frequently and is on their own, going down to the bar in the hotel every evening allows them to have some social interaction with others. There is nothing wrong with that initially; however, if it's the only way of passing time and if it occurs every night, this seemingly innocent practice can lead to too much alcohol being consumed.

Another excuse for employees drinking too much may be working long hours. Excessive alcohol consumption occurs particularly when there are extended periods of down time within an extra long workday. Sometimes employees who work long hours become bored. Having nothing else to occupy their time, they turn to alcohol. This may occur if an employee is working in a remote location off-site from his regular job. He then cannot get home and may only have a central area to socialise in. Or he might feel depressed and think that alcohol will drown his troubles or make him feel better.

Deadlines and workloads can cause an
increase in alcohol consumption

H45830

PART  Working under pressure

Workloads, long hours, shift work and harassment are just some of the things that can lead to stress and subsequently increased alcohol consumption.

What is stress?

The body has an inbuilt physical response to stressful situations. Faced with challenges or danger, we react quickly. Our body's reaction is to release hormones such as cortisol and adrenaline to help us do this. These hormones are part of the 'fight or flight' response. They affect our heart rate, blood pressure and metabolic rate. This results in

STRESS PROFILE

To help identify your level of stress, read the information below and circle the number that best describes you. 0 being type B through to 10 being type A.

Type B	Scoring Chart	Type A
1 Slow talker	0 2 4 6 8 10	Rapid talker
2 Easy going	0 2 4 6 8 10	Demanding
3 Listen well	0 2 4 6 8 10	Finish other's sentences
4 Do one thing at a time	0 2 4 6 8 10	Do many things at once
5 Express feelings easily	0 2 4 6 8 10	Bottle things up
6 Let things be	0 2 4 6 8 10	Like to change things
7 Gestures slow and rounded	0 2 4 6 8 10	Gestures quick and straight
8 Variety of interests	0 2 4 6 8 10	Work is only interest
9 Wait calmly	0 2 4 6 8 10	Impatient in queues
10 Delegate easily	0 2 4 6 8 10	Do everything yourself
11 Leave people be	0 2 4 6 8 10	Organise others
12 Even talker	0 2 4 6 8 10	Emphatic talker
	☐ ☐ ☐ ☐ ☐ ☐	= Total ☐

	Never Always	
13 Do you eat quickly?	0 2 4 6 8 10	
14 Do you walk quickly?	0 2 4 6 8 10	
15 Do you often work late?	0 2 4 6 8 10	
16 Do you set yourself deadlines?	0 2 4 6 8 10	
17 Do you hurry for appointments?	0 2 4 6 8 10	
18 Do you judge and measure things?	0 2 4 6 8 10	
19 Do you want exact details?	0 2 4 6 8 10	
20 Do you feel a sense of urgency?	0 2 4 6 8 10	
21 Do you feel guilty relaxing?	0 2 4 6 8 10	
22 Do you break the speed limits?	0 2 4 6 8 10	
	☐ ☐ ☐ ☐ ☐ ☐	= Total ☐
		Grand Total ☐

Stress Profile Analysis

Use your grand total to find out where you are on the type A / type B scale. The nearer you are to type B, the better for your health.

Low risk Type B	<100	101 to 149	150 to 174	175 to 220	High risk Type A

Stress often leads to drug or alcohol abuse

H46071

heightened, or stressed, state that prepares the body for optimum performance in dealing with the stressful situation.

Stress often leads to abuse of alcohol or drugs. These substances are used as attempt to self medicate. Obviously, stress affects just about everyone at some time in their life. As well as the emotional and psychological disruption it causes, it also causes stress-related medical problems which are becoming increasingly well recognised.

When we are faced with danger a challenge or pressure we often need to react quickly. In order to do this certain hormones are released:

- Cortisol.
- Adrenaline (known as epinephrine in the US).
- Noradrenaline (norepinephrine)
- Glucocorticoids.

These are the 'fight/flight' stress response hormones mentioned earlier.

If you were a zebra being chased by a lion your body would pump adrenaline into your bloodstream. The choice then would be to stay and fight or run as fast as you could. Whichever choice is made, the blood diverted from your digestive system and other non-vital systems would be pushed to your muscles to make you move faster. It would also enable you to withstand pain beyond normal limits. In these situations, vision becomes tunnelled; all focus is on the danger and all ordinary senses become numbed. The only focus *is* the danger. If such a situation occurs, you will be totally focused on fight or flight! Once the danger has passed, your body returns to normal. In the instance of the zebra, it would run away. When out of danger it would then quietly return to grazing with all body systems returning to normal.

Considering all this, and seeing how nature works, we as human beings have a problem:

- How does our modern lifestyle cope with this stress response?
- How do we cope with constant deadlines (stress), with office politics (stress), late-running trains (stress), etc?

Our bodies have quite simply not yet adapted or developed a separate stress response to modern day life. So often we have no way of effectively dealing with what amounts to ongoing stress.

Stress is a necessary part of life and keeps us protected and motivated, but when it is continuous, we are in danger of experiencing 'burnout.'

Experiencing stress over a period of time will start to cause physical and emotional or other mental damage. The essentially life-saving hormones that protect us and help us 'fight or flee' can – if pumped through our bodies in high doses and over extended periods of time – cause ulcers, depression, anxiety, auto-immune diseases and many other illnesses such as cancer. Also, when we are in 'hyper arousal' we then also become more prone to car accidents and emotional outbursts. In many ways this is like being on a drug-induced high, which, of course, it is! This self-manufactured high comes not from alcohol, but from the stress hormones being pumped through our bodies. However, as with drugs, this comes with negative effects. We burn out, generally not functioning to our best ability.

As a society at large we encourage stress. We value and esteem the workaholic. We set targets, deadlines and we strive for success. We view people who work hard and put in a lot of effort as successful and driven (stressed!). Material success is often the driver, and to this end, many people work beyond their physical and mental comfort level. This is all often to the detriment of our families, our minds (peace of mind) and our bodies.

How do we know when we are experiencing burnout?

Any of these symptoms or a combination would indicate that we need to be aware of being over stressed:
- Sleeplessness.
- Depression.
- Getting really angry and reacting out of proportion.
- Feelings of helplessness.
- Weight loss or gain.
- Frequent headaches.

How does stress influence the way we drink?

If we look at research we can see that people under stress (particularly ongoing stress) tend to drink in excess of what they would normally. People who are stressed tend to smoke more, drink more, and eat and exercise less than they should. People often drink in response to stress and the amount they drink is related directly to the amount of stress they are experiencing. Other factors are how much or little support they have and what sort of coping mechanisms they may employ.

So . . . what are the signs of stress?

Physical
- Headaches.
- Tiredness.
- Breathlessness.
- Palpitations.
- Muscle tension.
- Twitches.
- Indigestion.
- Nausea.
- Sweating.

Emotional signs
- Irritability.
- Depression.
- Anxiety.
- Cynicism.
- Lack of confidence.
- Low enthusiasm.
- Reduced self-esteem.
- Job dissatisfaction.

Maladaptive behaviour
- Insomnia.
- Restlessness.
- Accident prone.
- Increased drinking and smoking.
- Poor time-management.
- Inability to unwind or relax.
- Withdrawal from supportive relationships.

Cognitive functions
- Indecision.
- Worry.
- Muddled thinking.
- Poor judgment and concentration.
- Memory failure.
- Reduced attention span.

Can alcohol reduce symptoms of stress?

Some research shows that alcohol reduces stress, but other studies show that alcohol actually increases the stress response by stimulating the same hormones that the body produces when under stress. Overall, it's best not to turn to alcohol as a stress reliever. While we may feel we have relieved the stress, it is only a temporary fix.

Can stress cause alcoholism?

There is very little evidence to show that stress leads to the development of alcohol dependency. However, stress is strongly linked to alcohol abuse. Misuse of alcohol is often used as 'therapy' for life's problems. Stress is often associated with binge drinking. For alcoholics, or recovering drinkers, stress may lead to a recurrence of the problem.

Stress doesn't necessarily lead to alcohol dependency

H34126

Some early warning signs of stress which may lead to drinking problems
- Anger at anyone who makes demands.
- Self criticism.
- A sense of being overwhelmed.
- Cynicism, negativity and irritability.
- Chronic fatigue.
- Sleeplessness.
- Drinking more, or feeling the need to do so.

PART  Working and drinking don't mix

Tom Arnold, Sandra Bullock, Chevy Chase, Bill Cosby, Kris Kristofferson and Bruce Willis are all former bartenders.

Alcohol abuse is a problem that affects everyone. People who abuse alcohol are far less productive. Alcohol dependency can make someone despondent about work, particularly if it affects his health and the way he feels while on the job. Alcohol abusers also miss more work days than people who manage their drinking wisely or are abstainers. Again, it's due mainly to the physical effects they experience either during or after excessive drinking. They are also more likely to sustain injuries, which results in their filing more compensation claims.

Safety on the job

There are safety aspects to consider when examining alcohol consumption at work. Alcohol is obviously a bigger problem when looking at safety critical staff such as train drivers, bus drivers, pilots and doctors. The implications here are not only about personal safety but also about the safety of others. The far-reaching effects of alcohol dependency should be considered when other people are affected.

Accidents

Accidents are another area of concern as statistics show us that people who are under the influence of alcohol are more likely to have accidents than those who are not. There is little hard evidence that alcohol and work accidents are directly related. What we appear to have is a complex mix of factors that might lead to increased accidents. However, alcohol abusers are more prone to accidents than the moderate drinker or abstainer.

Absenteeism from work

Alcohol abuse causes a definite increase in absenteeism. Alcohol Concern suggests that up to 14.8 million working days are lost in the UK each year as a result of drinking. This translates roughly into 3 to 5% of all absences being drink-related. Long term sickness, unemployment and death due to alcohol are also estimated to cost some £2.3 billion a year (not counting short term illness, low productivity, etc). What is evident is that there is a strong link between alcohol and absenteeism.

If people drink large quantities of alcohol over weekends, they may feel ill on a Monday morning and possibly call in sick. However, the occasional hangover and not going to work are very different from 'problem drinkers.' Often though, real problem drinkers are able for a very long period to hide their problem. So what we might find in this instance is a long period where they are reliable at arriving at work and doing a job and then there may be a gradual increase in arriving late, leaving work early, etc, or if they binge drink, we may find specific periods where they are absent and this might increase in frequency. What is unclear is how long-term alcohol abuse affects work.

Why alcohol should be served at work

- No one would call in sick.
- Everyone would speak their own mind.
- No one would realise if there was a discrepancy in their payslip.
- No more pretending – who cares what management thinks!
- Increase in job satisfaction.
- Work would seem so much like a holiday, there would be less time taken off.
- Quality might not increase, but the perception of it would.
- Workers would have no need to make up excuses to stop for a drink after work.
- It would allow for a more open forum for ideas.
- Employees would no longer get drunk during their lunch breaks – they'd be there already!
- No more time wasted brewing coffee.
- Sick days would really be 'sick' days.
- The wife would have no reason to nag you for being drunk – it's all part of the job!

Photo: © iStockphoto.com, Marcin Balcerzak

Health and lifestyle screening can
be useful

Work-related intervention

Most people who have a drinking problem are still going to work
and managing to function on a reasonably normal level. So in
many ways the working environment is a key area in which to
help address alcohol abuse. Some of the methods that can be
used at work are listed below:

- Screening – health and lifestyle screening are often helpful
  both for the employer and the employee.
- Testing – would include drug and alcohol testing. How this is
  done, and on whom, is generally dependent on the company.
  Neither of the above methods is foolproof. They may act as a
  partial deterrent but it is not proven how effective they are.
  There are also potential human rights issues with regard to
  privacy.
- The 'buddy' system – this tries to create a culture in the
  workplace of concern where people are encouraged to
  approach each other if they feel there is a problem or go to
  their managers with their concerns. (If there is a treatment
  programme offered, it will be more effective if colleagues and
  family are involved.)
- Employee's assistance programmes have a value in that they
  will alert employers to any problems that can then be dealt
  with.
- Occupational Health – at work this can be a key place to help
  manage safety issues, health issues and run awareness
  programmes on alcohol and drugs.
- Health promotion – alongside the Occupational Health people,
  training and information and seminars on alcohol awareness
  can be extremely helpful and give people a better
  understanding of the long-term issues on alcohol abuse and its
  effects on those around the drinker.

There are some basic issues with interventions at work.
Managers may feel that they have not been trained properly to
deal with people who drink heavily – hence the need for
Occupational Health. And although someone might drink a lot, it
is often still felt that they are continuing to do their job well.

Actual enforcement of alcohol policy can cause severe delays
in production so often it is easier to turn a blind eye, particularly
if the alcohol-dependent employee is not slowing production,
quality, etc, at the moment.

Things to remember

- Up to 60% of problems at work caused by alcohol relate to
  people who have been on a bender the night before and not by
  people actually drinking on the job.
- Employees who drink heavily off the job are more likely to be
  absent due to hangovers, perform badly at work, or be
  argumentative.
- Heavy drinking is more likely to occur in male-dominated
  workforces such as construction.
- Workforces with a larger proportion of younger people are more
  likely to have a problem with alcohol.

In brief what we do know is that

- People with drinking problems use twice as much sick leave as
  others.
- They are more likely to cause injury to themselves.
- They are more likely to have missed at least two days of work
  in the last month.
- Members of an alcoholic's family report being negatively
  affected at work due to the alcoholic's behaviour at home.

Things we could do to help a colleague who has a problem

- Don't cover up for the person.
- Get help or at least suggest they talk to someone.
- Help establish a policy that would work for your company.
- Set up an anonymous support hotline.

Career

What it is that makes us want to succeed? Is that the real
question, or are the real questions:

- What holds us back?
- What makes us accept second best?

In Western society we are all very focused on career paths and
wanting to succeed. Many of us are not easily motivated,
successful and happy. Alcohol is one of the many ways that we
destroy ourselves and our careers. So often the pressure gets too
much, we fly too high and too fast and then, to deal with the
pressure, we drink!

What we all need to do is try to achieve a good work-life
balance and lead a life that makes drinking and working and
family fun.

There are many ways we can try to succeed and often we try
many of them but with no humour and no leniency. Here are a
few ways of helping you succeed without creating enormous
pressure. Remember, you have the potential to succeed without
resorting to drink or drugs.

Don't be afraid to ask
for guidance

HELP!

H46077

Here are some tips

- Allow yourself to ask for help and guidance.
- Let yourself look foolish or even stupid sometimes.
- Allow yourself to be different and stand out.
- Give yourself permission to succeed.
- Allow yourself to try.
- And allow yourself to fail.

We so very often do not allow ourselves to go forward. Instead we hold back and come up with many excuses. Yes, there are sometimes circumstances that can be trying but there is always a solution and we need to learn to explore those solutions and not restrict ourselves. For most of the time the things we want are well within reasonable bounds. We know that from the success others have achieved in the same situation. Therefore, there is no reason we cannot win.

Success is not necessarily about material gain. It can be about having a wonderful family, having respect, and doing a good job. It can be about not drinking to excess and causing others hurt. There are many goals we can set in life that can be considered success.

When we drink to excess we put a block in our way, we limit ourselves immediately and we stop our lives from moving in a positive direction. We put success on the back burner, and sometimes out of reach entirely. Take a moment to assess your own life. Is your drinking hindering from finding success?

Having a positive response to life and a philosophy that carries us through all major life events can be very useful.

Self perceptions

What is self-awareness? It is the ability to focus one's attention on oneself rather than the world around us. It is not selfishness, but it is having the ability to understand what is happening around us and being able to deal with it and relate it to ourselves in a personal and social way.

Again this links back to how we treat each other, how we behave, and whether we are able to say 'yes' or 'no' when needed.

Developing good self-esteem and self perception is key to preventing alcohol abuse. If you can develop that, you will be less likely to drown your troubles in the bottle should hard times come into your life.

Physical, emotional and spiritual health

- We can take care of ourselves and have a positive impact by eating carefully and nutritiously, as well as being physically active. We can learn to handle stress well and be aware of our feelings, which will alert us to depression or a desire to drink too much. We can be positive about all our attributes (difficult for an Englishman!). For those of us who can and do feel the need – spiritual well-being can offer satisfaction to us in allowing us to be forgiving, grateful, and at peace.

Attitude

- We can make our lives satisfying by enjoying what we do. By being responsible for our own well-being – taking care of our whole selves – and in that way not negatively affecting ourselves or others.

Communication

- There are a number of ways we can improve our sense of well-being. We can sense the world by being more observant as well retaining a sense of curiosity and using all our senses to enjoy the world around us. Good social interactions are important as well and can make life satisfying when you learn to have respect for others and try to help all around you in some way – constructive rather than negative.

Further reading

Dealing with Drink: Alcohol and Social Policy. Betsy Thom (Free Association Books, 1999)

Drugs and alcohol in the workplace: legal developments and management strategies. Victor Schachter (Executive Enterprises Publications, 1986)

Alcohol and Drug Related Problems at Work: The Shift to Prevention. Behrouz Shahandeh (International Labour Office, 2003)

Spirits and Demons at Work: Alcohol and Other Drugs on the Job. Harrison M. Trice, Paul M. Roman (ILR Paperback, 1979)

Films to watch

28 Days with Sandra Bullock
Shattered Spirits with Martin Sheen
Drunks with Faye Dunaway
Days of Wine and Roses with Jack Lemmon and Lee Remick

Alcohol and relationships

PART 5

Introduction and statistics

Wine has about the same number of calories as an equal amount of grape juice.

The Manhattan Cocktail, consisting of whisky and sweet vermouth, was invented by Winston Churchill's mother.

How many people are involved in the life of an alcoholic? Alcoholism affects everyone in the drinker's family, circle of friends, and co-workers. The problem is not only something the drinker has to deal with every day, but something everyone who is close to him, or comes in contact with him, also has to deal with.

Many of those affected by the drinker spend a lot of time and energy trying to 'fix' him: covering up for him, punishing him, taking responsibility for him. Living with alcoholism is similar to living on a merry-go-round where each family member, friend, employer, plays a role with the drinker. These behaviour patterns are like the script of a play, repeated over and over, centring on the person who drinks. Only by gaining an understanding of alcoholism can a player learn a new role and figure out how the disease has affected them. When this happens, and the person changes their behaviour, they can begin rewriting the script.

There is no guarantee that the drinker will change. However, the undesirable alternative is staying on the merry-go-round. Insanity can be defined as 'doing the same thing over and over and expecting different results'. Changing one's behaviour can be uncomfortable and very difficult to do, but it is possible and can be life changing.

The alcoholic family has been described broadly as one of chaos, inconsistency, unpredictability, unclear roles, arbitrariness, changing limits, arguments, repetitious and illogical thinking, and perhaps violence and incest. The family is dominated by the presence and the denial of alcoholism. The alcoholism becomes a major family secret, most often denied inside the family and certainly denied to outsiders. This secret becomes a governing principle around which the family organises its adaptations, its coping strategies, and its shared belief to maintain its structure and hold the family together.
Stephanie Brown

Half of all violent crimes are alcohol-related

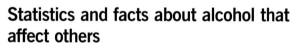

Statistics and facts about alcohol that affect others

Department of Health, 2004

- Between 15,000 and 22,000 deaths each year are associated with alcohol misuse, mainly resulting from cancer, stroke, accidental injury or suicide.
- Approximately one million children live in families where one or both parents misuse alcohol.
- 5.9 million people in England drink above the government's recommended daily guidelines.
- About 25% of children between the ages of 11-15 drink in excess of 10 units per week.
- 360,000 incidents of domestic violence are linked to alcohol misuse. This is approximately one-third of all domestic violence incidents.
- Half of all violent crimes are alcohol-related.
- 17 million days of absenteeism from work are alcohol-related.
- Around 70% of A&E attendances between midnight and 5am at weekends are alcohol-related.
- The loss of economy due to premature deaths from alcohol is around £2.4 billion each year.

PART 5

Effects on family/partner

Your relationship with anyone close to you should be nurtured and attended to on frequent occasions. When alcoholism enters the mix, it can seriously jeopardise an otherwise healthy relationship.

Often, because alcohol dependence progresses slowly and creeps up on the family, it is not recognised. Often the effect it is having on the family is not taken seriously enough. It is then difficult to differentiate between a normal family and an abnormal or malfunctioning family.

Just what is a healthy family environment?
The following ideals constitute a healthy family environment:
- All members of the family feel safe, loved, and cared for.
- There is trust, respect, and a good balance in meeting each member's needs.
- Parents are responsible and children are able to develop and grow.

Photo: © iStockphoto.com, Pascale Wowak

A healthy family environment is good for all members

49

Just what is a dysfunctional family?

The following loosely describes a dysfunctional family:

- Members suffer from anger, pain, fear, or shame that is ignored or denied.
- Members may suffer from emotional, sexual, or physical abuse.
- A family member may suffer from a chronic physical or mental illness causing undue stress on other members.

It is common for dysfunctional families to deny the existence of a problem. As a result, members of the family tend to repress their emotions and needs. They are often viewed as 'survivors'. They frequently develop behaviours that help them ignore or avoid difficult emotions. They tend to show little physical emotion, communication, and trust. Overall, the dysfunctional family members are inhibited and emotionally cut-off.

> 'The sway of alcohol over mankind is unquestionably due to its power to stimulate the mystical faculties of human nature usually crushed to earth by the cold facts and dry criticisms of the sober hours. Sobriety diminishes, discriminates and says no; drunkenness expands, unites and says yes'.
> Aldous Huxley

Denial, denial, denial . . . and we ain't talking about the river, Cleopatra!

When an alcoholic's partner or family members deny the existence of a problem:

- They usually develop a number of behaviours to maintain an illusion that the drinking is not affecting the family.
- Children in the family may assume the parenting responsibilities such as cooking, cleaning, and taking care of the younger family members.
- Partners/spouses may make excuses or even lie for the drinker when they have missed work or appointments because of a hangover.
- Family members may experience feelings of anger or resentment.
- Children may withdraw from friends or perform poorly in school.

It's important for families to admit that alcohol is causing a disruption in their lives and take steps to change it

Not only does denial occur with family members, it also occurs with the alcohol dependent person himself. In fact, denial is one of the key symptoms of alcohol dependency (alcoholism). The drinker often refuses to discuss his drinking and will dismiss it as an irrelevant issue. Frequently, he will become angry if pushed to discuss his 'drinking problem'.

Denying that there is a problem or refusing to discuss alcohol are clues that the drinker knows he has a problem. Frequently, as the drinking increases and begins to cause problems in his life, denial increases. Experts feel that this is purely a defence mechanism.

How is this possible?

If we look at the alcoholic's lifestyle, we begin to see that a support system – friends and family – is in place that enables him to continue denying the situation. This is often done with

> Drinking alcohol may incite violence – friends may assault you as you tell the same boring story over & over & over & over . . .

love and goodwill by those who pick up the pieces and carry on, who hide any mistakes and who generally support the person because he is fun, they love him, they think it is their duty.

By protecting the drinker, by making excuses, they prevent the person from facing the consequences of his actions. He experiences no real pain; he feels no direct effects of his drinking. The drinker, therefore, never learns how to accept and bear the *consequences* of his actions.

Note the following ways loved ones protect the alcoholic:

The alcoholic has...	He is faced with	Action taken
Been stopped for drunk driving	Losing licence/jail sentence	Wife/brother taking the blame
Punched a family member	Assault charges	Saying it was their fault/not pressing charges
Crashed a vehicle	Arrest/jail	Calling family to rescue/taking the blame
Not been able to go to work	Losing a job/livelihood	Calling in saying he is ill

While drinking increases a person's vulnerability, he can still believe he is fine because well-meaning family members, doctors, etc, rescue them from their 'consequences'.

Known as Enablers, these people effectively allow the alcoholic to continue in his denial until he is forced to face his habit due to enormous consequences that no one can rescue him from.

Improving the situation is possible. However, before a course of action may be taken, family members need a reason to pursue that course of action. The song of the rye about the effects of alcohol on the family – while a cute little ditty – reveals the devastation of alcoholism.

A song of the rye

I was made to be eaten
And not to be drank;
To be threshed in a barn
Not soaked in a tank;
I come as a blessing
When put through a mill;
As a blight and a curse
When run through a still!

Make me up into loaves
And your children are fed;
But if into drink
I'll starve them instead;
In Bread I'm a Servant
The eater shall rule;
In drink, I am Master
The drinker a fool!

Illustration: © iStockphoto.com, Ty Semaka

Is there anything we can do to improve the situation?
There are a number of ways to improve the situation. However, most family members need to realise how they are enabling the alcoholic before they have the strength and the knowledge to make a change.

If a member of your family were dependent on alcohol, how would you react?
Read on and find the number of ways people react.

The Provoker

This person punishes the drunk for his actions
She may leave him outside until morning and then ridicule him. On the other hand, she may put the hose on him! Basically, she lets the world know she is annoyed, upset and very angry. There is no question: everyone knows about it. Often this person threatens to leave and tells anyone who will listen how angry she is. She will hold the drinking against him, even for years to come.

The Rescuer

This person denies a problem and covers it up
The rescuer never lets the incident become a problem. Normally, she has been waiting for the alcoholic to return home. She opens the door for him and puts him to bed. If anyone mentions anything about his behaviour, she denies it, never acknowledging the possibility of a problem. However, as the problem becomes worse, the rescuer takes on more responsibilities and does extra jobs to cover any shortfall experienced through the drinker's behaviour. She protects him.

The Martyr

She lets all know how hard her life is
This person is ashamed of the alcoholic's behaviour and lets him know it by her choice of words and/or actions. She may say things like 'You have embarrassed us again'. Often this person will tell friends tearfully about the misery he is causing her. Or, alternately, she is so ashamed that she avoids all contact with friends and family, virtually withdrawing into a self-made isolation. The Martyr may become more miserable and depressed and withdraw from the world. Quietly, she will try to make the drinker feel guilty.

Do you see yourself exhibiting any of these behaviours?

Which one of these behaviours enables the drinker to keep drinking?

All of them!
- The non-drinking partner may fall into any one of these roles at one time or another.

Which one, in attempting to correct the drinker's behaviour, is actually adding to it?

All of them!
- It's easy to find ourselves locked into the alcoholic's behaviour. Responding to it often exacerbates it. At this point, we realise it's the moment to call *time out*!

- If he were always being rescued, why would the drinker admit he has a problem?
- If he never feels the actual consequences of his actions, why would he want to stop?
- The alcoholic tends to focus more on the reaction of the Enabler, than on the real problem: *his drinking*. The Enabler may successfully make the drinker feel guilt, but rather than quit, he will simply drink to avoid the guilt.

With that in mind, is there a correct reaction?

Of course, and the answer is simple – *do not react*
Instead, live as though everything is perfectly normal. Keep up your regular routine. For example: ready the kids for school, do your usual daily chores, keep going. While more responsibility may rest on your shoulders, do not allow his problem to disrupt you and your family's lives. This lack of reaction leaves the drinker to face his behaviour.

Any embarrassment, feelings of guilt, etc, are his feelings to face – *not yours*
Eventually, the pain of his behaviour will become too much for him to bear. The consequences will be too great for him to cope with. Finally, he will look for help. Until then, no amount of manipulation, tears or anger will do any good.

The issue of co-dependency

What is co–dependency?
Co-dependency is a behavioural and emotional condition that can affect a person's ability to have a normal relationship. Co-dependent behaviour is often found in dysfunctional families, sometimes passed from generation to generation. Occasionally referred to as 'relationship addiction', people with this behaviour tend to form a relationship that is emotionally destructive or abusive. Co-dependent behaviour is learned by watching and imitating other family members who display this type of conduct.

Who does co-dependency affect?
Often a family member, and sometimes even friends or co-workers of the drinker, are affected. Anyone who cares about or encounters the co-dependent is apt to become involved in his co-dependency.

Characteristics of co-dependency
- Difficulty in identifying feelings.
- Lack of trust in others.
- Problems with adjusting to change.
- A need to control others.
- Low self-esteem.
- An unhealthy reliance on relationships.
- Extreme need for approval and recognition.

How heavy drinking affects children in the family situation

Children who are raised in alcoholic families have different life experiences when compared with those raised in non-alcoholic families. However, children raised in other types of dysfunctional families may experience similar stressors, as do children in alcoholic families. Living with a parent who drinks generally makes a child unable to interact normally with other children. They also tend to have difficulty in maintaining appropriate learning levels. They may experience higher levels of conflict as well. Often the children of an alcoholic parent keep other family members at a distance. This may hamper their growth developmentally.

Unfortunately, children of heavy drinkers are more likely to become drinkers themselves than children of non-alcoholic parents. Research in this area is varied and often suggests that there is a genetic link. Although a child may be genetically predisposed to alcoholism, this does not mean he does not have a choice. There is also a strong link to learned behaviour.

Children's perceptions of how much and where their parents drink may influence their own drinking frequency. Interestingly, children become aware of their parents' drinking patterns at a very early age. Family interactions can also influence the child's risk of abusing alcohol. Families with a parent who drinks heavily have more negative interactions than normal families. Research shows us that almost one third of children who later become heavy drinkers had at least one parent who drank heavily. Parental drinking has also been found to influence adolescent substance abuse. Many times alcoholism leads to child abuse.

Some rules that children live by in alcoholic families are described well by the author Claudia Black:

- Don't trust.
- Don't feel.
- Don't talk.

Due to the alcoholic's unpredictable moods and broken promises, the child may grow up believing that others they encounter will become moody and untrustworthy. Likewise, because of the constant emotional pain of living with a heavy drinker, the child shuts off his emotions in order to survive. Most emotions experienced from drunken parents are abusive and erratic. The child mistakenly learns that showing emotion is not

acceptable. They seldom experience positive emotional occurrences.

Such a child's denial is a big part of his existence and there is the unexpressed belief and hope that 'if I don't talk about the alcohol, it won't affect me'. Also, there is the problem of never finding a good time to talk with the alcoholic parent. When he is drunk it is not a good time to talk, and when he is sober the child does not want to bring up such a painful subject. The child simply wants to forget, hoping the bad episodes have ended.

Each member in a family finds his own way of coping. Claudia Black and other authors describe roles that children often adopt in order to live within the dysfunctional family situation.

- **Hero** – These children try to make their family look 'normal' to the outside world. They are often high achievers and tend to be academically bright and successful. In order to do this, a child must pay a price. He denies his true feelings, thereby sensing he is an 'impostor'.
- **Placator** – These children try to keep the peace. They smooth over any arguments. They are in tune to other family members' feelings at expense of their own. Taking on the total emotional care of their family, they often wind up as adults in the helping professions – careers that reinforce their tendency to ignore their own needs.
- **Adjuster** – Due to family chaos, these children learn to adjust in abnormal ways. They try to avoid being noticed and keep out of sight, living 'just below the radar'. Once they become adults, they often feel that they are out of control of their own lives, just drifting along.
- **Scapegoat** – This is the child who becomes the focus of the family, who is used as an excuse for all that is wrong. He will be the one who gets into trouble, who expresses his anger through drug use, crime or alcohol. He also acts as the pressure valve for the family by creating a focus of attention through inappropriate behaviour. This diverts attention away from the drinker and allows denial to continue. It also gives the drinker an excuse for his addiction.

Alcohol misuse can be linked to physical abuse

Photo: © iStockphoto.com

PART

Effects on working relationships

The relationships within our working environments are an important part of our lives. We do not only work to earn money, but also to encourage social interaction. When we cultivate good relationships at work and at home we generally feel good about ourselves and enjoy being at work. If we start drinking heavily, over a period of time, both our home and working relationships become affected.

In addition to damaging our health, alcoholism may influence our performance at work as well as our professional relationships. There can also be an impact on productivity, career development and morale.

Symptoms in employees who have a drinking problem

- Excessive absenteeism – this usually shows up as frequent absences on a Friday or Monday, or prolonged lunch hours.
- Poor concentration and confusion – this often shows as memory lapses, difficulty in following through in tasks, and lack of attention to detail.
- Impaired productivity – the person's quality of work declines, they miss deadlines and have frequent errors.
- Avoidance of responsibility for one's actions – the person will give implausible excuses for not getting work done, blame others for mistakes and refuse to discuss problems.
- Poor working relationships – oversensitive to criticism, increased irritability, as well as experiencing complaints from co-workers about attitude and work quality.
- Mood swings – outbursts of anger, crying or laughter, as well as periods of depression, rage or anger.
- Poor personal appearance – smell of alcohol on breath, deteriorating dress habits.

Drinking alcohol may cause you to tell your boss what you really think of him.

From an employer's perspective

Alcohol consumption may well result in reduced work performance, damaged customer relations and resentment among employees who feel obliged to 'carry' the drinking colleague's responsibilities. Although there are no precise figures regarding the number of work-based accidents where alcohol is the cause, it is known that alcohol affects judgement as well as physical co-ordination. Drinking even small amounts of alcohol increase the risk of accidents.

Contrary to what many think, people with a drinking problem can work normal hours. Trying to ascertain how much alcohol employees consume can be a daunting task. However, acting to prevent problems before they occur can save time and money. Many companies nowadays have an active no drinking policy during work hours, including business lunches. Random testing has been instigated, as well, to enforce these policies.

What can you do to help?

As an employer
Find out if there is a problem. Is an employee:
- Drinking during breaks and before coming to work?
- Drinking during working hours?
- Getting drunk after work?

It may be useful to ask your employees what they know about alcohol and its effects on health and safety. Find out how they feel about drinking alcohol during working hours and be sure they know company policy related alcohol consumption.

Things you should be aware of:
- Any employee who is sick/absent frequently.
- Which departments have productivity affected by alcohol consumption.
- The status of your company's accident record.
- Disciplinary problems and if they are alcohol-related.

How to help
- Address work performance problems with the individual.
- Suggest professional help.
- Consult with the organisation's occupational health department, if appropriate.

As friends and co-workers
We might unwittingly become Enablers, which will only shield the drinker from experiencing the consequences of his actions – for instance by:
- Offering to call in sick for the person when the real problem is a hangover.
- Covering up mistakes for the drinker.
- Laughing at the anecdotes about the person's drinking rather than expressing our concern at the level of drinking.

We should:
- Help by refusing to cover up or protect the drinker.
- Refuse to make excuses and express concern at the level of drinking.
- Suggest seeking professional help.

Books to read

Understanding Co-dependency. Sharon Wegscheider-Cruse, Joseph Cruse (Health Communications, US, 1990)

Claiming Your Self-esteem: Guide Out of Co-dependency, Addiction and Other Useless Habits. Carolyn M. Ball (Celestial Arts, 1991)

Recovery from Co-dependency: It's Never Too Late to Reclaim Your Childhood. Laurie Weiss, Jonathan B Weiss, John Bradshaw (iUniverse.com, US, 2001)

Intimacy Factor: The Ground Rules for Overcoming the Obstacles to Truth, Respect, and Lasting Love. Pia Mellody (HarperCollins, 2004)

It Will Never Happen to ME. Claudia Black (Ballantine, 1991)

Safe Passage: Recovery for Adult Children of Alcoholics. Stephanie Brown (John Wiley & Sons Inc, 1991)

Another Change: Hope and Health for the Alcoholic Family. Sharon Wegscheider. Science and Behavior Books, 1981.

Guide to Recovery, A Book for Adult Children of Alcoholics. H. Gravitz and J. Bowden (Fireside; Revised edition, 1987)

The Struggle for Intimacy. Janet Woititz. (Health Communications, US, 1986)

About alcohol at work
Alcohol and Drug Related Problems at Work: The Shift to Prevention. Behrouz Shahandeh (International Labour Office/ILO/International La, 2003)

Spirits and Demons at Work: Alcohol and Other Drugs on the Job. Harrison M. Trice, Paul M. Roman (ILR Paperback) (Cornell University Press, 1979)

<aside>

Some things to think about

We must stop and examine our roles in a relationship before blaming alcohol
- How do we react to the other person's drinking?
- Could our reaction be part of the problem?
- Have we fallen into 'role playing' in the family?
- Is there anything we can do to improve the situation?

</aside>

<aside>

A sign that you are too drunk would be:
You engage in an argument with the objects on your desk . . . and you lose!

</aside>

Do I have a problem?

PART

What's the problem?

Drinking alcohol in moderation is not usually a problem. However, taking your consumption to the extreme may be. To many people, addictions seem to be pleasure-seeking behaviours. The cause of many addictions can be traced back to a wish to suppress or avoid emotional pain. They can be a way to escape reality or a way to hide from an emotionally empty life that is devoid of joy or happiness. Addiction can also be used as an escape from a relationship full of pain and sadness, such as abuse. Often early childhood trauma leads to addictive behaviours.

There are several stages in which alcohol dependence can be treated (see *Alcohol and work*). In this chapter, the focus will be more on treatment plans available. When your well-tuned engine starts to malfunction, action needs to be taken. Identifying and rectifying the problem will go a long way to keeping your body healthy physically, emotionally and mentally.

To find out if there is an alcohol addiction, we need to know the differences in various types of drinkers.

Just what is a 'drink'?

In the UK a 'unit' of alcohol is defined as 10 ml. Depending on the size and strength of the drink, many individual drinks contain more than one unit of alcohol. For instance:

A 125 ml (small) glass of wine at 12% ABV contains 1.5 units

A pint (568 ml) of beer at 4% contains 2.3 units

A single measure (25 ml) of spirits at 40% contains 1 unit – but the increasingly common 35 ml measure contains 1.4 units.

See the table on page 13 for more details.

Photo: © iStockphoto.com, Sherrie Smith

The social drinker knows what he is doing and isn't unintentionally embarrassing

The social drinker

- This is someone who drinks no more than 2 to 3 units of alcohol a day and does not become intoxicated. This person is unlikely to experience harm or harm others due to his drinking. You can invite this guy over and rest assured he is not going to embarrass you in front of your guests – at least not due to intoxication! He is a moderate drinker who is in control of his portions. He controls the drink – the drink does not control him. The amount of alcohol that can be consumed safely does vary by individual, but it is probable that most of those who drink this amount or less are in no way a threat to themselves or their families due to alcohol consumption.

The heavy drinker

- This is someone who consistently drinks more than 6 units of alcohol a day and without apparent immediate harm. You will often find him in a particular pub or bar. You could invite him over and not worry about him becoming falling-down-drunk. He may stop off every evening after work to have a few drinks on his way home. Then at home, he may have a few more, but without any observable differences in his behaviour.

The problem drinker

- This person has a problem – hence the term 'problem' drinker. He consumes enough alcohol for it to affect his behaviour. He experiences physical, psychological, social and occupational problems due to his drinking. His drinking affects his family life

Drinking alcohol is a major factor in unexplained rug burns of the forehead.

as well, and may lead to legal problems. At this point, a person's life starts to be disrupted due to alcohol. Steer clear of this guy – he will only cause trouble at your social gatherings.

The dependent drinker

- This is someone who has a compulsion to drink roughly the same, excessive, amount of alcohol every day. Over a period of time, he has an increased tolerance to alcohol in the early stages and a reduced tolerance later. This person will experience withdrawal symptoms if the alcohol is stopped; the symptoms will be relieved if he starts drinking again. Hanging around this guy will be nothing but heartache. For him, the drink is all-important. People, jobs, relationships all take a back seat to the bottle. While the dependent drinker may stop drinking for a period of time, he usually resumes drinking.

The ABC of alcohol

The problem with drinking is in drinking to excess. That's when a person's drinking gets out of hand and before he knows it, he is no longer controlling his drinking – his drinking is controlling him. Knowing this . . . why do some people drink to excess? Why do some form an addiction to alcohol?

The ABC is a simple way of figuring out how our minds affect our behaviour. It will allow us to understand the reasons behind our behaviour in different life situations. The person who drinks to excess may ask himself:

- 'Why do I drink?'
- 'Why do I find it so difficult to stop?'

Psychology can help. This is the science that studies human behaviour. Understanding an alcoholic's behaviour will help to you to understand why he behaves the way he does.

Just what is the ABC method? It is a way to analyse behaviour, to recognise it, and to modify it if necessary. 'A' stands for 'activators'; 'B' stands for (you guessed it) 'behaviour'; and 'C' stands for 'consequences'.

Activators

Those things that occur before the behaviour and that have an influence in the behaviour. They are the stimuli for a particular behaviour. This doesn't mean that the education we received, the country of our birth, the climate, and many other things do not affect behaviour; however, when we refer to a particular behaviour, these elements have less significant influence than other activators associated with the here and now. For example:

- You are hungry (A); you eat a sandwich (B).
- You hear the alarm clock (A); you get out of bed (B).
- You remember witnessing a car accident (A); you feel tense/nervous (B).

The activators determine a specific behaviour that occurs in one moment but not in another. By eliminating all the activators that influence a certain behaviour, we could deduce that the behaviour would not surface. Of course, in a normal life, it is not possible to eliminate all the activators. It is important to understand that the best way to eliminate a behaviour that you want to change is to identify the activators responsible for that behaviour and modify them.

> What you think you can do and what you think you can't do, you are quite correct.
> William James

External activators occur outside the person – e.g. a sound, another person's behaviour, the time of day, etc. *Internal activators* are thoughts or states of mind of the individual. All activators are stimuli that encourage dependent behaviour to rear its ugly head. However, they can also encourage the appearance of good behaviour. The key is to identify the activators that influence acceptable and unacceptable behaviour.

Behaviour

Behaviour is defined as anything a person does, how he acts, his conduct. Examples of behaviours are as follows:

- A person who is *speaking*.
- A person who is *listening*.
- A person who is *sleeping*.
- A person who is *eating*.
- A person who is *thinking*.

There are three differential types of behaviour: Thoughts, Feelings, and Actions. *Thoughts* are mental images or internal dialogues. *Feelings* are mood swings. *Actions* are the measures we take. These three elements are present around our behaviour. However, one of these elements can be more significant than the other two. For example: if a person feels depressed, the more important aspect to consider is the state of his mood, or his feelings. This would be the first thing to change.

Generally, we have the sensation that our external behaviour is under our voluntary control. In relation to our thoughts and states of moods (feelings), we don't see that so clearly. Sometimes we feel as if our states of moods depend on factors unrelated to us. We feel we have very little control over them. However, psychology teaches us that these three aspects of human behaviour are governed by the same laws as those that we are learning here. We can control our thoughts and feelings in the same way that we can control our actions.

Consequences

A consequence may be a positive or negative occurrence that happens due to behaviour. Logically, if the activators are what happen before the behaviour, the consequences are what occur later. The consequences, like the activators, have a definite influence on behaviour. You may wonder . . . how can that be? Especially if consequences come *after* a behaviour. Here's how: once the activators have influenced behaviour, consequences occur. Depending on these consequences, the behaviour may be strengthened, or reinforced, and the behaviour may ultimately become a habit. Or, depending on the consequences, the behaviour may disappear. Remember, consequences may be either positive or negative, and whichever they are will determine the life span of the behaviour.

- *Positive consequence.* When this occurs, the behaviour is reinforced, becoming stronger.

• *Negative consequence.* When this occurs, the behaviour becomes weaker and may eventually disappear altogether.

Say, for instance, you're at work. Your manager congratulates you for a job well done. This is an external consequence. On the other hand, if you tell yourself, 'I've worked well today,' it is an example of an internal consequence. As you can see, external consequences do not depend on us, while internal ones do. We can control the type, number, and the frequency of internal influences we receive. This can be of vital importance when we want to change our behaviour in a certain way. Do you see how effective this could be to the alcohol-dependent individual?

Is it possible to have a behaviour that has both positive and negative consequences? Hmmm . . . Yes! For example: We eat (C+ pleasure) (C- gain weight). We jog (C+ health) (C- fatigue, muscle pain). What consequences, in these circumstances, will affect the behaviour? Often the ones that occur first are the dominant influence. It does not seem to matter as to the intensity of their effects, what really matters is what happens at that first moment. It determines if behaviour will be reinforced or weakened.

Who, me? Exercise? Many people, even though they know going to the gym is good for them, will abandon it, allowing the negative consequence of pain and fatigue to dominate over the positive consequence of good health. Let's say a person starts cycling. The first thing he notices is that he is tired whenever he cycles. The benefits of health from cycling will appear if he sticks to it, but often he will become discouraged, giving in to the consequence of fatigue before he experiences the healthful benefits.

Roulette, anyone? In the case of a gambler, what is the first consequence he receives? Logically, he loses money. This is why most people do not become addicted to gambling; they never develop the habit. However, there are those individuals who are compulsive players. Just as there are people who will stick to cycling no matter how much fatigue they experience.

There is a different cognitive process that radically changes the situation. In the case of the cyclist, he may tell himself if he sticks to it, he'll be thinner, stronger, faster, in better health. In the case of the gambler, he may think to himself, 'I'll win next time.' The behaviours of cycling and gambling, in these cases, are reinforced.

You can now see the significance of internal consequences. By practising this, you are giving yourself a tool to understand the reasons for things which you previously thought 'just happen'. If you understand and use this basic principle, you can manage the behaviour you want to modify and be successful in achieving a desired outcome.

The earliest recorded patent application for a corkscrew in England was in 1795.

PART  # Warning signs

Now that we understand somewhat of what causes behaviours and ultimately consequences, let's find out what causes one to drink to excess.

We'll begin with cues. A cue is a specific sign that reminds a person directly about something – in this case, alcohol. The cue can induce you to drink. Examples of cues:

- Meeting with a drinking buddy.
- Your favourite team won! Let's celebrate! (Or they lost – let's drown our sorrows!)
- A drink in your hand.

Cues are significant keys to why a person drinks. They need to be recognised and controlled. Until they are recognised, they cannot be controlled. Many people do not realise there is an internal dialogue going on in which they justify drinking. Each person has a different approach in giving himself permission to drink:

- 'Just one more drink.'
- 'No one will know.'
- 'This will help me relax.'
- 'A drinking problem? No, not me.'

Recognising the cues will minimise the probability of alcohol abuse in the future.

Consequences, as mentioned above, are what happen after behaviour, in this instance, drinking alcohol to excess. There are short-term consequences and long-term consequences. Short-term usually occurs over a period from the time you take a drink to – maybe – the next day, generally no more than 24 hours. Long-term consequences may last from months to years.

Short-term consequences

- Pleasant taste.
- Talkative.
- Euphoria.
- Family disputes.
- Wasted money.
- Headaches.
- Feelings of blame.
- Nausea, vomiting.
- Hangover, sick feeling.
- Loss of appetite.
- Time off work.
- Unsociable behaviour.
- Isolation.

Notice that not all short-term consequences are bad. There are positive aspects to drinking, and it is the moderate drinker who enjoys more positives than negatives. However, see if you can find any positives in the long-term consequences below.

Long-term consequences
- Serious family problems.
- Problems in the workplace.
- Deterioration of personal health.
- Bad self-image.
- Social outcast.
- Financial problems.

Note that all the consequences for long-term drinking are negatives. When alcohol is abused, only bad things can happen. Not just for the abuser himself, but for his family, friends, and work mates.

Often, it's hard for people to admit they have a problem with alcohol. Many times other people notice the problem first. If they feel the drinker's problem may be interfering with their lives, they may comment on it. The drinker may be surprised, not realising – or possibly denying – he has a problem.

If you have to ask if you have a problem with alcohol consumption, chances are you do. If other people in your life have mentioned your alcohol problem, if it's that noticeable, you probably have one. If you have experienced serious consequences due to your drinking, and yet continue to drink anyway, that is a sign you have a serious alcohol problem.

Some people, after consuming excessive amounts of alcohol, have awakened the next morning with a major hangover – a negative consequence – and, as a result, have said, 'Never again!' And that's it. This person has no problem. However, if this person, having experienced such negative consequences, finds himself the next day – or a few days later – doing it all over again, he has a problem. His problem may be *alcohol abuse* or a worse *alcohol dependence* problem.

What's the difference?
- *Alcohol abuse* is a pattern of drinking behaviours that cause social problems, health problems, or both. The drinker is not dependent on alcohol, but uses alcohol irresponsibly, leading to negative consequences. He doesn't seem to know when to stop drinking.

- *Alcohol dependence* is a chronic disease. It's characterised by strong cravings for alcohol. The alcohol dependent drinker will constantly rely on alcohol despite serious negative consequences, and he will find he has the inability to limit his drinking. If he tries to stop, he will become physically ill due to withdrawal symptoms. He will also find that he needs to drink alcohol in greater quantities to feel its effects as his tolerance for alcohol increases.

> First you take a drink, then the drink takes a drink, then the drink takes you.
> Francis Scott Key Fitzgerald

> Diane and Sarah met for some drinks after work. After downing a few cold ones, suddenly – to Diane's surprise – Sarah fell off the barstool backwards, landing motionless on the floor. At Diane's gasp of horror the barman leaned over the bar and said 'When it comes to drinking at least she knows when to stop!'

Social problems, including relationships and responsibilities, at home or at work, are often the first signs of heavy drinking. Drunkenness may lead to car accidents, general falls, and/or physical violence. Disruption in the family is usually a good indicator of the seriousness of the problem. However, this is not always the case as family members sometimes cover up the problem for an extended period of time.

There are a number of questionnaires that are available to help diagnose whether or not a person has a drinking problem and to what extent. The following have been validated in primary care settings:

Alcohol Use Disorders Inventory Test (AUDIT)
- The AUDIT has ten questions and was developed for the World Health Organisation to assess alcohol use, including how often it has been consumed over the last twelve months.

Health Screening Survey (HSS)
- The HSS has nine items that examine lifestyle and asks questions about exercise, weight control, alcohol use, smoking, etc, over a three-month period.

Michigan Alcohol Screening Test (MAST)
- The MAST is most often used and consists of twenty-five questions which examine how alcohol has been used over the person's lifetime.

Cut down, Annoyed, Guilty, Eye-opener (CAGE)
- The CAGE is a simple four-question test that focuses specifically on drinking history. CAGE can be broken into the following sections:

C – the need to Cut down on your drinking
A – Annoyed when someone asks about your drinking
G – Guilty about your drinking
E – the need for a drink in the morning as an Eye-opener

The problems with CAGE and MAST are:

- They focus on lifetime problems, not on the present functioning of the person.
- There is an absence of 'alcohol use' questions.
- There is not enough focus on early problem drinkers.

Because of this, it is generally suggested that HSS and AUDIT are used, along with a few life questions and queries concerning drinking patterns.

AUDIT Questionnaire

Many people exceed the recommended safe alcohol limits through ignorance. If you find it hard to stick to the safe limits, try this Alcohol Use Disorders Identification Test (AUDIT) which helps screen for potential problem drinking.

Please RING your answer to each of the 10 questions

1 **How often do you have a drink containing alcohol?**
   (0)   Never
   (1)   Monthly or less
   (2)   Two to four times a month
   (3)   Two or three times a week
   (4)   Four or more times a week

2 **How many drinks containing alcohol do you have on a typical day when you are drinking?**
   (0)   1 or 2
   (1)   3 or 4
   (2)   5 or 6
   (3)   7 to 9
   (4)   10 or more

3 **How often do you have six or more drinks on one occasion?**
   (0)   Never
   (1)   Less than monthly
   (2)   Monthly
   (3)   Weekly
   (4)   Daily or almost daily

4 **How often during the past year have you found that you were not able to stop drinking once you had started?**
   (0)   Never
   (1)   Less than monthly
   (2)   Monthly
   (3)   Weekly
   (4)   Daily or almost daily

5 **How often during the past year have you failed to do what was normally expected of you because of drinking?**
   (0)   Never
   (1)   Less than monthly
   (2)   Monthly
   (3)   Weekly
   (4)   Daily or almost daily

6 **How often during the past year have you needed a first drink in the morning to get yourself going after a heavy drinking session?**
   (0)   Never
   (1)   Less than monthly
   (2)   Monthly
   (3)   Weekly
   (4)   Daily or almost daily

7 **How often during the past year have you had a feeling of guilt or remorse after drinking?**
   (0)   Never
   (1)   Less than monthly
   (2)   Monthly
   (3)   Weekly
   (4)   Daily or almost daily

8 **How often during the past year have you been unable to remember what happened the night before because you had been drinking?**
   (0)   Never
   (1)   Less than monthly
   (2)   Monthly
   (3)   Weekly
   (4)   Daily or almost daily

9 **Have you or has someone else been injured as a result of your drinking?**
   (0)   No
   (2)   Yes, but not in the past year
   (4)   Yes, during the past year

10 **Has a relative or friend or a doctor or other health worker been concerned about your drinking or suggested you cut down?**
   (0)   No
   (2)   Yes, but not in the past year
   (4)   Yes, during the past year

Procedure for scoring

Add up all the numbers you have ringed in the questionnaire. A maximum possible score is 40. A score of 8 or more is suggestive of problem drinking.
© *World Health Organisation*

Men who drink more than 21 units of alcohol per week and women who drink more than 14 units per week are considered 'at risk.' Also, anyone who binge drinks one or more times a week is considered 'at risk'.

If you're wondering if you have an alcohol problem, consider the following:

- Are you concerned about how much you drink?
- Do you drink at most social occasions?
- Do you feel you must drink to have a good time?
- Do you feel you have more courage when you drink?
- Do you keep a bottle in your car or close by in case you 'need' it?
- When things go wrong, do you have a drink to help you cope?
- Do you sometimes forget things that happened while you were drinking?

If you answered 'yes' to even one of these questions, you should be alert. While you may not have a drinking problem, you may be at risk of developing one should your habits increase or continue.

Signs that alcohol is a problem
- Insomnia.
- Being unusually suspicious.
- Accidents.
- Trembling hands.
- Erectile dysfunction.
- Loss of self-esteem.
- Blackouts or memory loss.
- Depression.
- Easily annoyed.
- Poor personal hygiene.

The three stages of alcoholism
Alcohol has been described as a disease of denial. It begins with drinking to deny life's problems and progresses to deny the drinking problem.

The early stage
This is the adaptive stage of alcoholism. Although we may not notice any outward behavioural changes caused by casual use of alcohol, such use is not safe as it often encourages the use of other drugs. Alcohol is known as a 'gateway' drug. Generally, anyone who drinks more than 21 units of alcohol per week, or more than 5 at a time on a daily basis, needs to be monitored. At this stage a person often drinks to change the way he feels. He starts by needing a drink to fit in with the crowd and have fun. Often, he pre-

drinks, or starts drinking before a party in order to attain a party mood. Sometimes he will be caught driving drunk and have his licence suspended. Blackouts or amnesia may occur but not to the point of actually passing out.

The mid stage

This stage involves a more frequent use of alcohol. The drinker finds that he needs to drink more in order to achieve the mind-altering euphoric effects of the alcohol. Not only is more alcohol consumed, but it is consumed more frequently. The drinker will have a preoccupation with getting a 'buzz.' Thoughts of suicide along with depression are common. At this stage, problems with law enforcement increase: fights, drunken driving, etc. Denial is very evident, as are a number of negative behaviours. Work and career problems may occur and lying to family, friends, and colleagues is common.

The drinker tends to fall into a trap – he needs the alcohol to feel good and when he is sober, paranoia sets in. This is the stage where families will begin to be dysfunctional. The drinker is not only creating problems for himself, but for those around him. This stage may last for years. Eventually, the drinker's low self-esteem is evident, people will withdraw from him, and he will feel ostracised by the world. He will often blame others for his problems and refuse to accept responsibility for what is going on. Often he will drink twice as much as those around him and also drink too fast. When he gets up in the morning, he may experience the 'shakes' until he has had a drink to steady himself. This is also the stage where erectile dysfunction (impotence) sets in.

The late stage

This stage is when the drinker experiences a 'need' to drink just to feel okay physically. He will feel powerless not to drink. Physical damage to his body will occur, including damage to the liver, heart, and brain. His immune response is lowered and he may be plagued with pneumonia. Also, blackouts are common. By now, the drinker's family life has pretty much disintegrated. However, the drinker has developed an 'I don't care' attitude. This can be directed toward the problems in his life or to his life in general. He really doesn't care if he lives or dies.

At this stage, it may take serious consequences to put him on the road to recovery. However, depending on the severity of the drinking and the physical effects on the drinker, he may be institutionalised by his family or doctor. Family, friends, and colleagues have largely given up; the drinker's plight seems hopeless. Many alcoholics do not reach this last stage. They usually die from accidents at home or on the job, or from physical complications due to their alcohol dependence. They have a 15 to 20 year shorter lifespan than does a recovering alcoholic or non-drinker. The physical complications are generally from cirrhosis, respiratory diseases and malnutrition. Suicide is often a prime cause of death.

The twenty most important questions you'll ever ask yourself

In order to determine if you are at risk, consider the following questionnaire.

- Do you lose time from work due to your drinking?
- Is drinking making your home life unhappy?
- Do you drink because you are shy with other people?
- Is drinking affecting your reputation?
- Have you ever felt remorse after drinking?
- Have you had financial difficulties as a result of your drinking?
- Do you turn to inferior companions and environments when drinking?
- Does your drinking make you careless of your family's welfare?
- Has your ambition decreased since drinking?
- Do you crave a drink at a definite time daily?
- Do you want a drink first thing in the morning?
- Does drinking cause you to have difficulty sleeping?
- Has your efficiency decreased since drinking?
- Is drinking jeopardising your job or business?
- Do you drink to escape from worries or trouble?
- Do you drink alone?
- Have you ever had a loss of memory as a result of drinking?
- Has your GP ever treated you for drinking?
- Do you drink to build up your self-confidence?
- Have you ever been to a hospital or institution on account of drinking?

If you answered 'yes' to more than two or three of these, there is a strong possibility that you may be an alcoholic.

Alcohol hell – hangover intensity scale

Level one
You wake up with a lot of energy. You're experiencing no pain and no feelings of sickness. You're pleased that everything is functioning okay. However, you are super thirsty. You feel like you could drink ten gallons of water and still feel parched.

Level two
You look just fine but your brain is on cruise control without the cruise. You chug a ton of coffee, but your gut is craving a high-carb breakfast. Your digestive system is going hay-wire.

Level three
You're experiencing a slight headache and your tummy isn't feeling quite right. Your productivity is poor. You've downed all sorts of liquids and that dehydrated feeling still hasn't gone away.

Level four
You're reeling from a throbbing headache that intensifies every time you turn your head. You're wearing sweaters on your teeth, and you feel like you're going to puke. It's an effort to speak and make sense. You wish to god you'd never gone out the night before. Life sucks.

Level five
Your head feels like you have a second heartbeat inside. Throbbing headache is too tame a phrase to describe what you're

feeling. Now there are two layers of sweaters on your teeth. Even breathing hurts. You're not sure what happened last night or how you got home. And who the heck is that stranger snoring in your bed? Death looks pretty good right now.

If you've experienced any of these, don't despair . . . there is a solution
A wise man once said, 'Time heals all wounds.' In time, and without a repeat of the excessive drinking that caused the hell you're in, the symptoms will disappear and life will go on.

Hangover types
Not only are there levels of hangovers, but there are different types of hangovers. See if any of these sound familiar:

The 'I should've had dinner' hangover
This one usually occurs towards the end of some Friday Happy Hour where your lightweight co-workers are taking off for home right as your unemployed, well-rested, recently-fed college chums are arriving and offering to buy you shorts. 'Later,' you promise yourself, 'I'll duck out for a bite.' You never do, since the increasing alcohol makes you think your stomach is full, not only of whimsy and mischief, but nutrients. What a deceptive magician alcohol can be! Suddenly morning hit you in the ear drums like a snare drum sound check. Probably the most painful of all hangovers, it's an especially frustrating species when you realise that it could have been easily avoided.

- *Cure:* Soda water, peanut butter, The Simpsons, apple juice.
- *Avoid:* Coffee, aspirin, TV commercials, household chores.

The 'I shouldn't have mixed' hangover
It's hard and dull to just drink one thing all night. But if you mix, you're in for trouble. Maybe you start with cocktails, have wine with dinner, then after-dinner drinks, then shots of peppermint schnapps and god-knows-what-else, you poor fools. The hangover is roughly proportionate to the number of drinks you've mixed, divided by the increase in sugar per shot. Try to drink a glass of water as you cross each threshold to a different kind of spirit. Avoid

Photo: © iStockphoto.com, Laura Tomlinson

late-night shots of strange spirits that drunken out-of-towners try to coerce you into trying. The main symptoms of this particular hangover will be a pounding headache with a subsequent urge to challenge people bigger than you to fights over nothing.

- *Cure:* Ibuprofen, coffee, water, fresh air, sex.
- *Avoid:* Beer, loud music, oversleeping, sugary breakfast cereal.

The 'I shouldn't have gone out' hangover

It was only going to be a few quick drinks after work but due to some warp in the time-space continuum (or abduction by aliens) you re-enter your drunken body at about 1am and realise that it's been on alcohol auto-pilot for the past six hours. Not having remembered the last thirteen drinks, you feel a bit ripped off and have a few more that your brain insists will be okay, despite compelling physical evidence that you've probably had enough. You feel surprised at your mouth's inability to form a coherent sentence, and your sense of balance has been inexplicably taken offline, which also surprises the heck out of you as you fall off your stool (again). You arrive home at 2:30am and climb into bed.

Sleep comes instantly, as you were fighting it all the way home in the taxi. You get about two hours' sleep and then the noises inside your head wake you up. You notice that your bed has been cleared for takeoff and is flying relentlessly around the room. No matter what you do, you know you're going to chuck. You stumble out of bed and now find that your room is in a yacht

under full sail. After walking along the skirting boards on alternating walls knocking off all pictures, you find the toilet. If you are lucky, you will remember to lift the lid before you spontaneously explode and wake the whole house with your impersonation of walrus mating calls. You sit there on the floor in your undies, cuddling the only friend in the world you have left – the toilet – randomly continuing to make the walrus noises, spitting, and farting. Help usually comes at this stage, even if it is short-lived. Tears stream down your face and your abdomen hurts. Help now turns into abuse and it usually goes back to bed, leaving you alone in the dark.

With your stomach totally empty, your spontaneous eruptions have died back to 15-minute intervals, but your body won't relent. You are convinced you are starting to turn your body inside out and swear that you saw your bum come out your mouth on the last occasion. You lie there, cold and shivering, with eruptions now occurring at 1-hour intervals. It is now dawn and you pass your disgusted partner getting up for the day as you climb into bed. She condemns you again for trying to get into bed with bits of dried vomit in your hair. You reluctantly take her advice and take a shower, get back into bed, and wait until you feel well enough to eat on the following day. The mention of alcohol makes your stomach churn.

- *Cure:* Not much – this one just takes time, and the effects will linger for about a week.
- *Avoid:* Most things, particularly the people you chewed out while on auto-pilot.

The 'I've been drunk for 14 hours' hangover

This is the one you should be proud of because it shows endurance and pacing. You probably had a high-protein dinner and didn't mix alcohols. You went the distance and in the late afternoon of the next day, you feel something, but it's not as bad as it could be. The reason? You're still wasted! By the end of the day, your real hangover will take over unless you act wisely.

- *Cure:* Swimming, vitamins, lying in the sun, more alcohol.
- *Avoid:* Staying inside in front of the TV all day.

The 'I've been drunk for 3 days' hangover

Now you're wading into serious waters. You partied in grand style Friday night, got an early start Saturday, but managed to still go the distance. Now it's Monday and you're no longer able to speak. Your eyes are beetroot red. Ghost beatniks pound your skull like a bongo. You can't eat, and sleep won't help. You have no concept of time. Day, night, all you know is that you are conscious. You pass out on the bathroom floor and wake up to somebody whispering your name, but you can't turn around to see them.

- *Cure:* House cleaning, scratchy country blues CDs, a long shower, religion, re-hab, French cinema & cuisine.
- *Avoid:* Cheap beer, TV repeats, parents, crowded places.

PART  Routine maintenance

Sooner or later, if you drink to excess, it will affect that finely-tuned vehicle known as your body. When that happens, maintenance or repair is in order. Often, the help we require is more than we can handle on our own. For times like this, we must seek outside help. This is not always easy, particularly if we have been in denial about our problem. However, realising we need help is the first step. Another difficulty is if we are living with someone who is dependent on alcohol. If that is the case, it's best to seek support and link up with others in our situation before seeing if we can get the drinker to acknowledge their problem.

Generally, your GP is the first port of call. If you are the alcohol abuser, he will ask you a number of questions, including how well you are sleeping and whether your work/family is being affected by your drinking. He will give you a few blood tests to check out liver function and your general well being. Your blood pressure will be checked as well. He will then determine the best method of treatment to help with your alcohol problem.

Your doctor will check liver function and blood pressure

H46075

Brief interventions aim to identify a real or potential alcohol problem and to motivate the person to deal with it. The focus in brief intervention programmes is on nondependent drinkers; whereas an alcohol-dependent drinker would need a more extreme programme. A brief intervention has the potential to significantly decrease alcohol usage and the problems associated with heavy drinking. They are less expensive than visits to casualty units for alcohol-related injuries, and are less expensive than rehabilitation programmes. A number of countries, including the UK, Canada, and Australia, as well as others, have begun implementing brief intervention programmes for alcohol problems into their health care systems.

Drinking problem solver

Symptom	Fault	Action Required
Drinking fails to give taste and satisfaction; beer is unusually pale and clear	Glass empty	Find a friend who will buy you another beer
Drinking fails to give taste and satisfaction; and the front of your shirt is wet	Mouth not open when drinking or you missed your mouth with the glass	Buy another beer and practise in front of the mirror, being sure to drink as many as you need to get it right
Feet cold and wet	You've either spilt your beer or emptied your bladder	Carefully keep the open end of your glass pointed to the ceiling or stand next to nearest dog, complain of its lack of house training and demand another beer as compensation
Floor blurred	You're looking through the bottom of your empty glass	Find a friend who will buy you another beer
Floor moving	You are being carried out	Complain loudly that you're being kidnapped
Everything has gone dark	The pub is closing	PANIC

Now, seriously, if you suspect an alcohol problem in yourself, your first step should be to visit your local GP. He or she will usually:

- Ask questions, possibly using one of the questionnaires mentioned earlier.
- Advise you how to come to grips with your problem and how to explain to your family the seriousness of your problem, including treatment and detoxification.
- Suggest a detox plan to help you withdraw from alcohol slowly if you are a heavy drinker.
- In some instances, put you on medication to help you stay off the booze.
- Discuss the need to stop or curtail your drinking.
- Discuss what drinking standards are and why they are beneficial.
- Encourage and support you in your efforts to improve.

If you are a friend or family member of an alcoholic, your GP will usually:

- Talk to you and assess your level of unhappiness, suggesting you seek support via counselling or other alcohol-related support agencies.

Drinking alcohol may lead you to believe you are a Master of Kung Fu.

- Offer information about helpful options for the drinker and how to go about seeking them.
- Listen sympathetically and try to assess the severity of the drinking problem.
- Possibly offer to talk to the drinker for you.
- Suggest the person in question be given a full medical assessment as a start to diagnosing his problem and opening up dialogue.

Brief interventions may cause the drinker to experience stages of change, rather than a quick change all at once. Here are the steps generally taken by the drinker:

Pre-contemplation
- The drinker is not thinking of changing his habit and may not be aware of the health consequences of continued drinking.

Contemplation
- The drinker is aware of his alcohol-related behaviour and its consequences, but still may not want to change.

Preparation
- The drinker is at a stage where he is aware of his alcohol problem and is planning to do something about it.

Maintenance
- This is when the drinker has reduced his drinking or in some cases eliminated drinking alcohol completely.

Types of drinkers

There are generally four very broad categories that everyone falls into. They are:

Abstainers
- 'No, thanks, none for me.' These people do not drink at all.

Low-risk drinkers
- 'That's enough for me.' These people drink minimum amounts of alcohol and seldom go over the limit. They don't drink at all for at least two days out of the week.

High-risk drinkers
- 'Just one more, to calm my nerves.' These people drink more than three days a week and 'need' their drink.

Alcohol-dependent drinkers
- 'Pour me another.' These people cannot stop drinking. They feel a need to drink if they experience any stressful situations at all. Drinking elevates their mood and they need this to mask their depressive and miserable feelings.

Help yourself

There are ways that a person can help himself if he just has the will and strength. The following is a list of things to do before you take your next drink:

- Postpone the drink.
- Stay away from the alcohol's location.
- Call someone who does not drink.
- Go for a walk or exercise.
- Visit friends or family.
- Write a list of all the negatives that happen when you drink.

If you are too embarrassed to talk to your GP, or if you don't have one, you may want to access the Internet and see what alcohol help lines and centres are available in your area. Remember that finding the resources is not the same as following through. It is an all-important step to acknowledge you have a problem, and to follow up with getting help. Friends can be very encouraging and supportive and may even go with you to a consultation if you need them.

You may find that seeking help in your community is preferable. Some churches will offer help to alcohol and drug-dependent people. Generally, treatment plans are broken down to fit the level of dependency. Wherever you find support, take advantage of it. You'll be glad you did. Getting help is the first step to getting your 'vehicle' running smoothly again.

For further information

www.alcoholics-anonymous.org
www.alcoholconcern.org.uk
www.healthatoz.com
www.recovery-man.com
www.alcoholscreening.org

Abstainers do not drink at all . . .

. . . while alcohol-dependent drinkers cannot stop

Always do sober what you said you'd do drunk. That will teach you to keep your mouth shut.
Ernest Hemingway

Alcohol relapse and prevention programmes

PART

Treatment

Alcohol dependence does not have just one specific treatment. With all treatment programmes, the main focus is relapse prevention. This will be discussed in further detail later in this chapter. The treatment options are varied and are greatly dependent on the alcohol abuser, his doctor, and funding.

Treatments come in the form of:

Medication
• To help with the withdrawal symptoms and to help control cravings.

Therapy
• To help improve coping skills; to help learn ways to avoid tempting situations; to help avoid stress which can lead to relapse. The goal of therapy is to enable the person to understand why he abuses alcohol – along with behaviours that lead to heavy drinking – and to put into place tools to help him avoid relapse.

Support groups
• To give encouragement and accountability, and self-help.

Hospitalisation
• This occurs in extreme alcohol dependency to detoxify the body. It is used in conjunction with one or more of the other treatment methods listed above.

Any treatment, of course, is ineffective unless the individual realises he has a problem and needs to change it. The first step is in admitting he has a problem.

> Drinking may make you wake in a pool of vomit, wondering where you are.

Therapy alone and in groups can help

Photo: © iStockphoto.com

Stress and alcohol

Everyone has had and will have stress in their lives. It can come in many forms, both good and bad situations: the birth of a child, a divorce, financial difficulties, increased job responsibilities, the death of a family member. Whatever the situation, bringing heavy drinking into the mix is never a good option. Many people think that they can 'drown' their troubles in alcohol. However, while they may forget them for a while, the troubles will still be there when they sober up, possibly compounded by their heavy drinking. During stressful periods, try to make a greater effort to keep alcohol consumption in check. If not, the problems will only increase, possibly in the form of alcohol dependency. Behaviour therapy may be needed to help an affected individual handle difficult situations.

Even though a number of people have tried, no one has yet found a way to drink for a living.
Jean Kerr

The three most commonly used forms of therapy

12-Step Facilitation Therapy
- This therapy is based on the well known Alcoholics Anonymous (AA) approach and gives the alcohol abuser twelve activities that should change during recovery.

Cognitive Behavioural Therapy
- This type of therapy is based on helping alcohol abusers develop strategies to cope and recognise high risk situations.

Motivation Enhancement Therapy
- This therapy helps to motivate alcohol abusers make changes in their behaviour.

All of the above therapies have been proven effective in reducing the abuser's alcohol-related problems.

Inpatient and outpatient treatments are two other ways of finding help with alcohol-related dependence and are discussed further in the next Section, *Intensive treatment*.

Self-help programmes

Many people find self-help programmes helpful in gaining control over their use of alcohol, or as a means of continued sobriety after a more intensive form of treatment. The most well known of these is Alcoholics Anonymous (AA).

AA was founded in America by two alcoholics in the 1930s. There are group meetings daily, and these are facilitated by group members. Attendance is voluntary and membership is absolutely free. Members can attend as many or as few meetings as they like, as this is a self-directed therapy support network. Group members support each other and the 'buddy system' was developed to help each person work through their problems with support from a sponsor or 'buddy' who is always available to them. All group members need to have been dependent on alcohol and be facing or have faced similar issues. Being a 'buddy' is a powerful commitment, as this person often acts as a 'lifeline' for recovering alcoholics, who may feel the need to call for support during times of stress or crisis, when there may be a great risk of relapse into alcohol use. Therefore, most programmes stress that each member wait for a period of time before choosing their 'buddy', since one must feel that the person of their choice will be someone they would be comfortable calling at any time, if cravings to drink are strong.

AA uses a 12-Step Programme which was developed by the earliest members of AA. With the programme the person follows the basic ideals:

1 Abstinence-based personal recovery program from the substance of choice eg, alcohol.
2 Admits their own powerlessness over the substance or behaviour.
3 Turns their fate over to a higher power (as you understand or believe).
4 Follows steps to examine the effects their behaviour has had on their life.
5 Accepts responsibility for damage caused to others and to make amends.

The 12 Suggested Steps of Alcoholics Anonymous

1 We admitted we were powerless over alcohol – that our lives had become unmanageable.
2 Came to believe that a Power greater than ourselves could restore us to sanity.
3 Made a decision to turn our will and our lives over to the care of God as we understood Him.
4 Made a searching and fearless moral inventory of ourselves.
5 Admitted to God, to ourselves and to another human being the exact nature of our wrongs.
6 Were entirely ready to have God remove all these defects of character.
7 Humbly asked Him to remove our shortcomings.
8 Made a list of all persons we had harmed, and became willing to make amends to them all.
9 Made direct amends to such people wherever possible, except when to do so would injure them or others.
10 Continued to take personal inventory and when we were wrong promptly admitted it.
11 Sought through prayer and meditation to improve our conscious contact with God, as we understood Him, praying only for knowledge of His will for us and the power to carry that out.
12 Having had a spiritual awakening as the result of these steps, we tried to carry this message to alcoholics, and to practice these principles in all our affairs.

The 'higher power' part of the 12-step programme can be an integral part of many AA groups; however, this is often amended, as it sometimes offends people who do not subscribe to a particular religious faith.

AA can be found in most cities around the world. It is completely free and welcomes all who have a common area of need. It does not always work for everyone and often requires the person to have already attended a clinic for 'drying out' and therapy. It works best as a support network and in preventing relapse through the help of others through the 'buddy system.'

SMART (Self-Management and Recovery Training)

This is based on principles of CBT (Cognitive Behavioural Therapy). It aims towards abstinence with a focus on self reliance and self-directed change, as well as self-empowerment, and teaches specific tools and techniques within a 4-point programme which consists of:

- Coping with urges.
- Problem solving (managing thoughts, feelings and behaviours).
- Enhancing and maintaining the motivation to abstain.
- Getting and sustaining a lifestyle balance, i.e., balancing momentary and enduring enjoyment and satisfaction.

Women For Sobriety (WFS)

This organisation focuses specifically on the needs of women alcoholics whose recovery in AA had been found to be less successful than for men. The structures for this organisation are based on:

- Thirteen positive statements to encourage spiritual and emotional growth with and emphasis on positive reinforcement as well as cognitive strategies and relaxation techniques which help women come into good contact with their own bodies, to heal and restore.
- Weekly meetings in small groups with a structured format for confidential discussions.
- Recognition that the psychological needs of women are different from men.

Drinking may make you wonder what happened to your bra.

Cognitive Behavioural Therapy (CBT)

This is a way of talking about how we feel about ourselves and the other people around us. It looks at the affects our thoughts have on us, and is used to help change how we think (cognitive) and what we do (behaviour). Changes can help us feel better, and the beauty of CBT is that it focuses on the present and on how to change our state of mind in the present. It does not necessarily address or focus on the causes of our distress but looks to dealing with the presenting problem or problem behaviours. Thus CBT is a valuable tool for the recovering alcoholic in dealing with everyday stressors without the use of alcohol as a 'buffer.'

CBT is often used to help people who are suffering from:

- Phobias.
- Depression.
- Anxiety.
- Addiction.
- Obsessive compulsive disorder.
- Some eating disorders.
- Post Traumatic Stress Disorder (PTSD).

How does it work?

Very simply CBT can make sense of problems by breaking them down into smaller parts, which makes it easier to see how they affect you. The parts can be:

- Actions (drinking too much).
- Thoughts (depression).
- Physical feelings (pain, hurt).
- Emotions (sadness, overwhelming grief, guilt, or anger).

Each one of these areas can affect the other area. Each interlinks and can affect what you do about it. Seeing more clearly, how our actions are directly related to our emotions can help to us to handle these emotions in healthy, non-destructive ways.

What we all often do is create a vicious circle/cycle, which leads us in ever increasing negative feelings and situations.

CBT can help us break this cycle by changing the way we think as well as our behaviours and feelings. By seeing things in broken down parts we can see things more clearly and it is then so much easier to change them. The aim of CBT is to get the person to a point where they can work out their own way of dealing with their problems realistically, practically and most of all effectively.

How effective is CBT?

CBT can be extremely effective in treating addiction as it breaks problems down and helps come up with really practical ways of changing behaviour. With addiction this is normally of paramount importance.

What are the negative aspects of CBT?

If you are having trouble concentrating it can be hard to get the hang of the therapy but then that would be the case for most psychotherapies. It can also be difficult to talk about our feelings in a way that allows us to easily separate them out. Today, most alcohol treatment programmes use some form of CBT in their process and it is steadily becoming a treatment of choice.

Sign you are too drunk: You can't focus with both eyes open.

ALCOHOL RELAPSE AND PREVENTION PROGRAMMES

Intensive treatment

Inpatient treatment

This usually involves a period of time in a clinic or hospital and can be anything from a few days to a few weeks (short-term) to a few months or a year or more (long term). This sort of treatment is generally for people who lack social networks, who haven't managed with outpatient programmes or who suffer from additional problems, be they psychological or medical.

Generally these sorts of treatment include some form of alcohol education as well as different types of therapy. You can usually find this sort of treatment offered as a residential treatment programme which recommends abstinence or a hospital/medical clinic which uses medication as part of the drying out and treatment programme. Detoxification from alcohol is a part of this inpatient treatment and is discussed below.

It has been found in numerous studies that a combination of inpatient programme and then support via an AA type support group worked better than AA alone or inpatient treatment alone.

Detox

What is detox and how do we go about it?

For many individuals who are considering entering intensive treatment for alcohol dependency, detoxification can be a very frightening concept, one that may even deter some from people from seeking treatment. It is important to understand the detoxification is a 'good' thing, as the definition below indicates.

With today's level medical understanding of alcohol dependency and its affect on the brain and body, physicians are very knowledgeable regarding proper methods of helping a patient through the detoxification process. It is very important to remember that painful and even dangerous withdrawal is very likely to occur if an individual with a history of heavy alcohol usage attempts to withdraw without medical intervention. The purpose of inpatient treatment is not only to help in the long-term goal of abstinence from alcohol, but also to make the process of detoxification as easy for the patient as possible, through the use of medications and psychological counselling.

Alongside this, a mental and physiological readjustment needs to take place. This is what is meant when people talk about entering 'detox'

Alcoholism requires detoxification before one can begin treating the person and helping them on the road to recovery. Whilst the person has any residual alcohol in their body they will continue to have cravings and it will be very difficult for them to achieve concentration and start recovery.

The severity as well as the intensity of the withdrawal symptoms when discontinuing alcohol depends on the drinking history of the individual and their usage. Each and every alcohol detox programme is unique to the person in terms of time, medication, etc.

The definition of detoxification is one which allows for the treatment of addiction to drugs or alcohol which is intended to rid the body of the addictive substance(s).

It is important when deciding to detox that this is done with the help of proper medical or health care supervision, especially in the instance of heavy drinking.

If you just want to cut down and are a moderate drinker, the risks are minimal, but care should still be taken and your nutrition will still need to be monitored, since long-term use of alcohol depletes the body of vital nutrients.

There are two types of detox: Non-medical and Medical.

Medical
This covers a wide variety of detoxification techniques used by the medical profession. They range from simple observation by professionals while an individual detoxes naturally, to medical intervention which may include tranquilisers or other drugs that reduce the symptoms caused by withdrawal of the drug of choice – alcohol in this instance.

Which medical detox procedure is used depends on a number of factors including which type of drug is being detoxed, eg, alcohol, the severity of the problem and also the philosophy of the treatment centre. Terms we will hear in these settings are:

Rapid detox, medical detox, etc. Generally the most successful detox programmes deal with both the mental and physical symptoms of the withdrawal. The time necessary for an alcohol detox can be anything between 3 to 14 days. Benzodiazepines and anticonvulsant medications are some of the more common drugs used. Persons seeking treatment for alcohol dependency may wish to discuss the method of treatment of the particular programme they are entering prior to their admission.

Non-medical
This refers to the fact that the body will rid itself of drugs, including alcohol, if no more toxic substances are introduced. This is sometimes known as going cold turkey.

Symptoms of alcohol withdrawal can include sweating, rapid pulse, increased tremors, autonomic hyperactivity, nausea, vomiting, sweating, anxiety and mental withdrawal. Depending on the person's alcohol history these symptoms can be quite severe and might even include hallucinations and in extreme cases the possibility of grand mal seizures. Therefore medical intervention is always advised when discontinuing long-term use of large quantities of alcohol.

Autogenic training in detox
This is a relatively new way of treating and enhancing the non-medical detox process and works on the assumption that if one can calm the autonomic nervous responses and reduce anxiety the person will be able to come through the detox more quickly and with some anxiety reducing tools.

Autogenic training has an advantage over normal psychotherapeutic models in that it is a tool that can be used by the person wherever they are, once training has been done.

What is autogenic training?
Autogenic training is an extremely effective self-help therapy – a unique mind and body therapy which gives self-control over health and well-being. Who wouldn't want that?

The emphasis remains on allowing the self-righting mechanisms of the body to regain homeostasis (homeostasis is the inclination to rebalance the organism. In this instance the body seeks to create balance).

- Autogenic, which means 'self-regulation or self-generation', refers to the way in which your mind can influence your body to balance the self-regulative systems that control circulation, breathing, heart rate, and so on.
- Autogenic training allows you to control stress by training your autonomic nervous system to become relaxed.
- Simple mental exercises allow relaxation to take place, in turn allowing rebalancing or 'homeostasis' to take place.

The method is self-administered and taps into the system's remarkable capacity for healing and re-balancing of both physical and psychological functions.

Once mastered, AT is always available without the need for a therapist or any equipment.

The combination of using a deep relaxation programme, with the added dimension of emotional release when required, gives an individual a remarkable tool-kit for maintaining emotional and physical equilibrium for the rest of their lives.

Outpatient treatment programmes
This is treatment which takes place outside a medical or residential setting and can include things like alcohol education, individual counselling, group therapy, and education on all aspects of health and family related to alcohol misuse and dependence. Outpatient treatments can vary in their services offered and you can have:

- Day programmes in hospitals which will give continuity in treatment.
- 8-hour sessions which will include a variety of therapies focusing often on relapse prevention, communication, looking at self-esteem and managing anxiety.

Or:

- Night classes where a person can attend after work and can still lead a relatively normal life whilst still having the advantage of treatment which is ongoing and supportive.

Finding a treatment programme that suits you or your partner can be difficult as a number of factors will come into the decision. These can be as simple as availability of facilities, whether there is private health insurance coverage, factors such as pregnancy, young children being involved, the need for other medical treatment, etc. All of these will be taken into account, and to a large extent advice can be given on this from one's GP or health workers.

PART  **Turning over a new leaf**

Earlier sections have detailed various treatment options for alcohol abuse. Turning over a new leaf and beginning a new life of sobriety involves learning to look at life in a new way. With the proper treatment regimen, and support through AA or other self-help programmes, success can be achieved.

Prior to entering into a treatment programme, many individuals may view their use of alcohol as a form of harmless recreation. Ever heard of drinking games? If so, you may be using these games as a way to justify overindulging in alcohol or to disguise an alcohol problem.

Time to get serious = No More Games

When you are playing drinking games, they may seem like quite a bit of fun, and of course, since the point of the game is to encourage consuming large quantities of alcohol, it is easy to hide a potential or actual alcohol dependency problem behind them.

Relapse

Many thousands of people receive treatment for alcohol dependence each day around the world. For the majority of people battling with alcohol dependence the only rescue is complete abstinence. However, even with the best will in the world and all the support, people do have slip-ups and relapse. Research has shown that approximately 90% of recovering alcoholics will slip up at least one time in the first four years of recovery.

It does not mean a person cannot recover even if they have to attend a programme again or review treatment.

Once a person has been through a treatment process and is on the way to recovery a whole lot of new and exciting life events await them. However, at first it is important to focus on some practical things.

Changing habits

There is a saying that 'old habits die hard,' well with the road to recovery – it's not a matter of old habits dying hard, but a must that they change.

Once again it is a good idea to look at and review on a regular basis your habit-breaking plan.

- Re-examine on a regular basis your reasons for cutting down or stopping drinking.
- Be aware of any dangerous situations – high risk for drinking. Remember how to cope if in these situations.
- Learn to avoid high risk situations wherever possible, or at least plan how you will behave if you know you will be facing one.
- Always have a helping and supportive friend around if you can.
- Have a number of people you can rely on to call if you feel vulnerable and about to relapse.
- Change where you used to go during your drinking days.
- Do not set yourself up.

Increased self-awareness means protection.

Changing or maintaining friendships

This is always a difficult task as once you are sober you are faced with the reality of who your friends are, and what you need to do. Often, our drinking buddies have to be 'dumped' and our more reasonable friends informed that we are not drinking and need support and encouragement around this area. You will be amazed at how many people will say how they too should stop drinking, have stopped drinking and or admire you your determination.

Work functions can be difficult to start with but if you have attended a good programme you will have been taught how to order drinks that don't get people quizzing you about what you are drinking. You will still be able to fit in with the crowd and not feel uncomfortable. In today's world there are a lot of people who don't drink at work functions, and more and more there is a trend towards not drinking at lunchtime or during working hours, so this should be a lot easier.

Increasing self-awareness

As we come back to the world and face it sober, so too do we find that we are very aware of ourselves as a person, and all of those who surround us.

There seem to be 4 major areas that set us up for relapse.

- Personality traits.
- Substitute addictions.
- Narrow view of recovery.
- Failure to see danger signs.

What can prevent relapse is being more self-aware. Recovering alcoholics need tolerance to recognise their harmful personality traits – some self-exploration and learning through therapy or AA groups is useful.

It is also helpful to look for signs of substitute addictions such as compulsive shopping, eating or gambling to name a few. Some replacements as simple as enjoying eating or working a bit more are important, but anything excessive is worth being concerned about

Constant work on personal growth, a sense of purpose in life and developing good relationship is part of the road to recovery and enhancing self-awareness.

If a friend or relative relapses it is very important that they understand that it is part of the process, that we can still get back on track and that if we are aware, monitor our behaviour and change old habits we will manage. The recovered drinker needs to be able to monitor changes, to their thoughts and emotions and their behaviour that precedes a relapse in order to be aware of it for the future.

'I began to understand that self-esteem isn't everything; it's just that there's nothing without it.'
Gloria Steinem

Increasing fitness

Exercise repairs the damage done by alcohol and gives you more energy, less stress and tension. Confidence also tends to rise as you look and feel better. Exercise such as cycling, walking and hiking can include the whole family so has the bonus of creating and enhancing a positive family life. Before starting exercise it is vital that you check with your doctor what exercise is appropriate.

Laughter is vital as it increases all the good hormones and fills you with a sense of lightness. Find enjoyable activities that make you feel happy or make you laugh. When you go to the cinema, try watching comedies rather than dramas, or purchase humorous novels to read.

It has also been found that aerobic exercise reduces depression symptoms and negative moods. One reason appears to be that aerobic exercise, like laughing, affects endorphins or chemicals in the brain known as endogenous opiods, which can create a sense of pleasure and possibly help reduce alcohol cravings. It is also recognised that people who participate in a regular form of exercise learn new skills which help build self-esteem and gain a sense of control over their environments.

Aerobic exercise reduces depression and negative moods

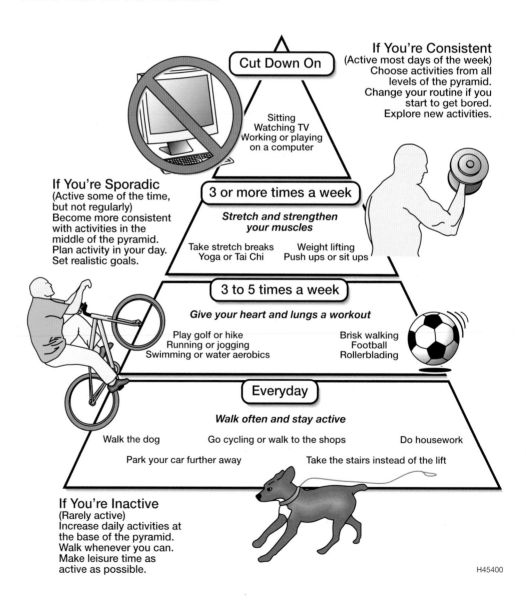

Cut Down On

If You're Consistent
(Active most days of the week)
Choose activities from all levels of the pyramid. Change your routine if you start to get bored. Explore new activities.

Sitting
Watching TV
Working or playing on a computer

If You're Sporadic
(Active some of the time, but not regularly)
Become more consistent with activities in the middle of the pyramid. Plan activity in your day. Set realistic goals.

3 or more times a week

Stretch and strengthen your muscles

Take stretch breaks   Weight lifting
Yoga or Tai Chi   Push ups or sit ups

3 to 5 times a week

Give your heart and lungs a workout

Play golf or hike   Brisk walking
Running or jogging   Football
Swimming or water aerobics   Rollerblading

Everyday

Walk often and stay active

Walk the dog   Go cycling or walk to the shops   Do housework

Park your car further away   Take the stairs instead of the lift

If You're Inactive
(Rarely active)
Increase daily activities at the base of the pyramid. Walk whenever you can. Make leisure time as active as possible.

H45400

Feeling positive; enhancing your self-esteem

Have the vision to dream BIG!

There are many ways a person can change negative thoughts and self-criticism to more realistic and positive thoughts. Focusing on all of them at once may be overwhelming, but focusing on a few at a time and reminding yourself of these positive approaches regularly can change your self-esteem.

Accentuate the positive

- Instead of focusing on what you think are your negative qualities, accentuate your strengths and assets. Maybe you felt nervous and self-conscious when giving a presentation at work, but maybe your boss and co-workers respected you for getting up and trying.

Avoid exaggerations

- Correct your internal voice when it exaggerates, especially when it exaggerates the negative. Try to avoid thinking in extreme terms: 'I always make that mistake' or 'I'll never get that promotion.'

Accept flaws

- Maybe you did get nervous and blow that presentation at work – so what? Talk to your boss about what went wrong, try to address the error in the future, and move on. All people have flaws and make mistakes. Your boss, co-workers, friends, family, postman, and favourite movie star have all made mistakes. They've forgiven themselves; so can you!

Nip negative thoughts in the bud

- Sometimes putting a stop on negative thinking is as easy as that. The next time you start giving yourself an internal browbeating, tell yourself to 'stop it!' If you saw a person yelling insults at another person, you would probably tell them to stop. Why do you accept that behaviour from yourself?

Accept imperfections

- Perfection is a high goal to aim for – you don't need to start there or even end there. Make doing your best your ideal – what more can you realistically do? Focus on what you've gained from the process and how you can use it in the future. Avoid focusing on what wasn't done or should have been done differently. Allow yourself to make mistakes and then forgive yourself. Try laughing instead of criticising.

Don't bully yourself

- 'Should have, could have, would have . . .' Try not to constantly second guess yourself, criticise yourself for what you *should* have done better, or expect too much from yourself. Don't put standards on yourself that you wouldn't expect from others. It's great to want to do well, but expecting yourself to be perfect (which is impossible) and then punishing yourself when you fail is a vicious cycle. Using expressions like 'I should have' is just a way of punishing yourself after the fact.

Replace criticism with encouragement

- Instead of nagging or focusing on the negative (in yourself and others), replace your criticism with encouragement. Give constructive criticism instead of being critical ('maybe if I tried a different approach next time, it would be even better' instead of 'I didn't do that right.') Compliment yourself and those around you on what you have achieved ('Well, we may not have done it all, but we did a pretty great job with what we did.')

Don't feel guilty about things beyond your control

- You are not to blame every time something goes wrong or someone has a problem. Apologising for things and accepting blame can be a positive quality, if you are in the wrong and if you learn and move on. But you shouldn't feel responsible for all problems or assume you are to blame whenever someone is upset.

Don't feel responsible for everything

- Just as everything is not your fault, not everything is your responsibility. It's okay to be helpful, but don't feel the need to be all things (and do all things) for all people. This is taking too much of a burden on yourself and limiting those around you. Let others be responsible for themselves and their actions – you shouldn't feel responsible for their happiness.

Do feel responsible for your feelings

- Just as you can't 'make' other people happy, don't expect others to 'make' you feel happy or good about yourself. In the same way, they shouldn't make you feel guilty or bad about yourself. You create your own feelings and make your own decisions. People and events may have an affect on your emotions, but they can't dictate them.

Treat yourself kindly

- People often feel more comfortable treating themselves in ways they wouldn't consider treating others. Do you criticise yourself with terms like 'stupid', 'ugly' or 'loser'? Would you use those terms to describe a friend? Remind yourself that you deserve to be treated as well as you treat others. Do something nice for yourself sometimes – either in thought (give yourself a compliment) or action (treat yourself to a nice dinner or new book. NOT A DRINK!)

Give yourself a break

- You don't need to be all things to all people or please everyone. Give yourself permission to decide you're doing the best you can. Remind yourself when you're doing things well – don't wait to hear it from someone else.

Choose the brighter side of things

- You can choose how to interpret comments and events, so try for the more positive interpretations. If someone says, 'You look good today,' don't ask yourself, 'What was wrong with the way I looked yesterday?' Accept compliments graciously (Don't ask yourself why you haven't been complimented on something else or why they haven't complimented you before.) Look at temporary setbacks as opportunities for growth.

Forgive and forget

- Try not to hang on to painful memories and bad feelings – this is a sure-fire way to encourage negative thoughts and bad moods. Your past can control you if you don't control it. If you can, forgive past wrongs and move on. (Don't forget that forgiving yourself is an important part of this process, too!) If you have a hard time forgiving or forgetting, consider talking through your emotions with a good friend or counsellor, but try not to dwell. It's important to work through things, but you can't let the past determine your future.

The magic mirror technique

This is a very powerful way of setting personal change in motion that only takes a few minutes to do. Imagine that you are standing with a full length mirror behind you. Now imagine all those aspects of yourself that you no longer want, reflected in the mirror behind you. For example, you might imagine yourself as overweight (perhaps eating junk food); or as a smoker (perhaps with cigarettes in your mouth); or as somebody who is unfit, unhappy, or whatever. Spend a minute to allow yourself to notice all sorts of details about this image. Now imagine a full length mirror in front of you, and in this mirror see reflected the 'new you' that you want to become. Make this image as bright and realistic as possible. Imagine that you are smiling and happy, more confident, fitter, slimmer. You can imagine the clothes you are wearing, the way that you stand, the way you breathe and move. When this image is at its best, imagine that you step forward into it, and that you truly become the 'new you'. Notice how good you feel; be aware of how different you feel. Allow yourself to really enjoy this experience, to really live it. When you are ready, open your eyes again, and allow yourself to come back to the here-and-now. To really reinforce this work, repeat the whole process five more times, opening your eyes between each repetition.

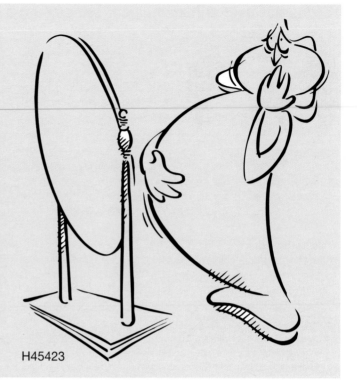

H45423

Focus on what you can do, not what you can't

- Avoid 'can't' thinking or other negative language. If you say something often enough, you may start to believe it, so keep your statements positive, not negative. Don't be afraid to seek help in accomplishing things, but remind yourself that you don't need approval from others to recognise your accomplishments. Focus on what you're able to do. Remind yourself of all your capabilities and positive qualities

These are just a few ways of gaining self-esteem and positive feelings, all of which will contribute to staying sober and confident. These same points apply to all people, drinkers or not, and are well worth remembering.

Beginning a new sober way of life takes courage, and involves using the tools learned in whatever treatment regimen one has chosen, to view stressors in a different light, and to use these tools to react in healthy ways to deal with stressful situations.

Further reading

The Power of Positive Thinking. Norman Vincent Peale (Ballantine Books, 1996)

The Positive Principle Today. Norman Vincent Peale (Fireside; Fireside edition, 2003)

Enthusiasm Makes the Difference. Norman Vincent Peale (Fireside; Fireside edition, 2003)

You Can If You Think You Can. Norman Vincent Peale (Fireside, 1987)

Tough Times Never Last, But Tough People Do! Robert Harold Schuller (Bantam, 1984)

Any of the Lawrence Block novels about Matthew Scudder which tell of an alcoholic getting on with life.

Taking the lift and not the stairs

Photo: © iStockphoto.com, Josef Kubicek

PART 8 **Awareness**

Just how much do you drink? Do you know . . . really? Being aware of your own alcohol consumption is all-important in determining if you have a problem with alcohol or if you are at risk of having a problem. Learning to recognise the triggers that lead to drinking is a significant factor in awareness. This is especially crucial when recovering from alcohol dependency. Very early in sobriety, news articles, television commercials, smells, songs – almost anything – can be a threat to your recovery. These triggers can very well cause a relapse. However, the longer a person abstains from alcohol, the easier it is to abstain. Not to say it will be easy – just easier. Therefore, while certain influences may trigger a strong desire for alcohol soon after treatment, their hold on the recovering person will lessen with time. The desires may still be there, just not as intense.

If you are looking for an excuse to drink anything will do.

Below are six statements that show triggers to drinking alcohol and how these triggers sneak up on us:

- I will always have cravings (triggers) for alcohol.
- When I am craving (trigger) alcohol, I cannot function.
- The craving (trigger) makes me use alcohol.
- If the craving (trigger) gets too intense, drinking alcohol is the only way to cope with the feeling.
- The craving (trigger) is a physical reaction so I cannot do anything about it.
- I am always having cravings (trigger) for alcohol.

Take note that all of the above statements have an element of truth in them. More importantly, however, they can be used as triggers to begin drinking again if one is not aware of them.

It is imperative to learn how to combat the triggers to drinking. In order to do that, we need to:

- Resist the urge.
- Make healthy choices.

Sometimes stressful situations lead to alcohol consumption in order to cope. These can act as a trigger. For a good example, see the statement above that reads: *If the craving gets too intense, drinking alcohol is the only way to cope with the feeling.*

Symptoms of stress affect us every day. We may experience very little stress, or our stress levels may be elevated to the breaking point. Stress may be physical, emotional, or mental. Have you experienced any of the symptoms shown in the chart below?

Making the decision to cut down on your drinking or to cut it out completely is a big decision. Once you've chosen to follow the path of sobriety, you should follow these steps:

- Recognise: Know where you're coming from and where you're going.
- Avoid: Be aware of the 'triggers' that can lead to a relapse.
- Cope: Learn how to cope with your new way of life.

Drinking alcohol may cause periods of time to disappear.

Physical	Emotional	Mental
Heart pounding	Moody	Forgetfulness
Headaches	Irritability	Loss of concentration
Sweaty palms	Depressed	Poor judgement
Indigestion	Anxious	Disorganised
Skin disorders	Lack of sense of humour	Fuzzy perception
Shortness of breath	Abrasive	Confused
Holding the breath	Hostile	Lack of interest
Cold hands	Nervous	Mathematical errors
Sleeplessness	Emotional	Stopped thinking
Fatigue		Negative self-talk
Nausea		
Diarrhoea		
Tight stomach		
Tight muscles		
Pain		

An important thing to remember is that recalling negative consequences becomes an effective way of reminding yourself of the benefits of remaining abstinent and the negative effects of drinking. Sometimes it may be painful to remember the hard times you went through because of your drinking. However, it is a necessary part of successfully reaching your goal of abstinence and sticking to it.

Keeping a card in your wallet or purse is a great idea. On one side of the card, you should list all the reasons you want to stay abstinent. Give good reasons – believable reasons – real reasons. When you feel a weak moment – and you will – re-reading this list of reasons can encourage you and keep you strong. On the other side of the card, list the negative consequences of drinking. Be brutally honest. You know the negative consequences – you've experienced them. Draw from your experiences and use these to remind yourself of how drinking alcohol caused pain in your life, and possibly – most probably – in the lives of others. Re-reading your list of negative consequences will remind you how drinking alcohol is detrimental to a successful, sober life. Now, you'll, of course, want to look at the card each time you are tempted to drink. However, don't stop there. Read over it daily to remind yourself to resist temptation when it rears its ugly head.

Being aware of your alcohol problem often comes due to questions you've considered and answered honestly about yourself. Some things to consider when assessing your situation are:

- Have you ever received professional treatment for your drinking?
- Do you drink to overcome shyness around people or to build self-confidence?
- Do you awake wanting a drink or crave one at the same time each day?
- Is drinking affecting your family life or job situation?
- Do you drink when you are around certain people or do you drink alone?
- Do you drink to escape from real or imagined problems?
- Once you sober up, do you feel remorse for having drunk too much?

Now, most of what you've read in this chapter refers to you, if you are the one with the drinking problem. But what if the drinker is not you but someone close to you? And what if he is unwilling to face his problem? This can be a problem for you and those who care about the person who drinks.

Realise that the person you care for is a sick person. Look at him as someone that can be helped with treatment; his irrational conduct and drinking habits are, therefore, symptoms. There are several steps you can take. The main thing is – for your own peace of mind – to get support. Certain groups are geared toward the support of adults and children that are being affected by those who drink. A group may help you realise you are not responsible for the drinker abusing alcohol, and that you need to make sure to take care of yourself, whether or not the drinker chooses to get help for his problem.

Are you talking to me?

You may find that positive self-talk is an invaluable way of dealing with cravings for alcohol. While the phrase 'self-talk' may be new to you, the art of self-talk is not. Think about it. We all do it everyday. We verbally beat ourselves down or lift ourselves up. Let's say you're faced with a decision:

- Should I buy that car or this one? You reason within yourself the best choice, you weigh the pros and cons, and you make a decision.
- Or perhaps you're in a clothes shop. Which looks best: the blue jeans or the black ones?
- You peer into the cupboards in your kitchen. What should you make for dinner?
- You're preparing to go out on a date. Should you wear your hair gelled or styled?

Every day decisions must be made, from the small mundane ones to the greater life-changing ones. Some decisions you make so often, they are almost automatic. Others require deep thought, concentration and consideration.

For many people, a variety of automatic thoughts accompany their cravings for alcohol. These thoughts can be so deeply ingrained, the person may not even be aware of them. A key point to remember is that thoughts directed toward cravings almost always have a sense of urgency, as in 'I have to have a drink *now*!' In order to cope with these cravings, it is important to recognise these automatic thoughts. Recognising them will help you not give in to them. And that is the ultimate goal. Once you identify them, you can combat them by using positive self-talk, such as:

- Challenge the thought: 'I'll be okay, even if I don't have a drink.'
- Normalising the craving: 'The craving is uncomfortable, but a lot of people have it and it's something I can deal with without drinking.'

Now, think about this for a moment. Challenging the thought gives you power over the craving. It enables you to strengthen your resolve either not to drink at all, or to drink only in moderation. You are in control, the drink is not. Think of other reaffirming statements you might use when challenging the thought, or craving, for another drink. It may help to minimise the craving in your own mind and maximise the power you have over it. In normalising the craving, you recognise the fact that yes, it is there, but you are not the only one who has ever had to deal with it. You face the fact that many people each day are experiencing the same temptations, and many are successfully overcoming the temptations. If they can do it, why not you? Tell yourself this. Self-talk yourself into believing it. Why? Because it's true.

PART  Responsibility

The buck stops here. A significant step in combating alcoholism is to take responsibility for your alcohol consumption.

Clarifying goals
- Are you ready to change?
- How do you feel about abstinence?
- What is your sense of target goals and problems?

Stop!

Before you read any further, take a moment to list the reasons *why* you want to change. Now, don't read further. List them now. Really. Right now.

Finished? Now, read over the list. Is there anything you've left out? Okay, let's move forward.

Next, list the reasons why you do not want to change. (No, that's not a misprint, you read it right.) Be honest with yourself enough to list all the reasons why you do not want to cut down or stop drinking alcohol. Think about it.

Now, read over your list. Is there anything you should add?

Make an honest list of why you want to change

In thinking of both of your lists, travel down the road of your past experiences. Travel as widely through your thoughts as you can. Sometimes it's hard to be honest – even with ourselves. Even on a list that no one will see but us. However, it's important that you don't censor anything that comes to mind. The issues that pop up may include effects of alcohol on your long-term and/or short-term health, your state of mind, your family and relationships, your social life, your work, your money, your time, and even your problems with the law. Again, it is imperative that you be completely honest. This list is for your eyes only.

Once you've honestly completed your two lists, it is time to assess them. Look closely at both of your lists and compare them. Which one gives the most reasons? If the reasons for change do not outweigh the reasons not to change, you may find it difficult to succeed. Difficult, yet not impossible. Just be aware of that fact.

During the next week or so, keep a journal. This is simply a tool to help you know exactly where you are in your consumption of alcohol. Again, this is for your eyes only. In your journal, you'll want to chart where you drink – the physical location, be it a pub, a friend's house, a restaurant you frequent, or at home. You'll also want to chart when you drink – the days of the week and the times of the day. And you'll want to chart with whom you drink – your friends, co-workers, family members, or if you drink by yourself. Last – but certainly not least – chart the cost and consequences of your drinking, both negative and positive. Again, be honest, even if it hurts.

Chances are, during this time period, there will be both positives and negatives. During that week or so, you just need to chart these criteria. Afterwards, pull out your journal and scrutinise it. Flip through it and see where you were in the beginning and how that period of time progressed. Check out the negatives and positives and make a mental note. This will help you focus on the scale of the task at hand. It will also show you where some possibilities for change might lie.

Next, your task is to decide what your goal should be. It's all up to you. You are the one in charge. Ask yourself:

- 'Do I want to stop drinking completely?'
- 'Do I want to merely cut down on the amount I am drinking?'

If, after considering these questions, you are still unsure, don't stress over it. Simply take it a step further. Get out your trusty pen and paper and list the pros and cons for each alternative. Again, honesty is key. Here are some questions to help you get started:

- What benefit will I gain by not drinking?
- What benefit will I gain by drinking only in moderation?
- What problems can I eliminate by giving up alcohol?
- What problems can I eliminate by cutting down on alcohol?
- How much money will I save?
- What are the pros and cons of the effects on my health?
- How will eliminating alcohol completely affect my family and relationships?
- How will cutting down on alcohol consumptions affect my family and relationships?

Once you have your lists, read over them. Consider them carefully. The more knowledge you begin with – your lists – the greater are your chances for success in reaching your goal.

Drinking alcohol in moderation is where many people choose to start. Research has shown that you can avoid more severe problems related to alcohol is you take steps early enough. Let's say you decide to drink in moderation rather than eliminating alcohol from your life completely. What does 'moderation' mean to you? How much alcohol would you consume? In other words, what would moderation mean to you in practice?

Obviously, there is no right or wrong answer. The answers to those questions vary from person to person. Also, the problems alcohol is causing in your life would be a deciding factor in determining what amount of alcohol is moderate. Again, look at your list – the list you created of reasons why you want to change. Looking at it, in all honesty, try to work out what level of use would be likely to free you of these problems.

Some helpful suggestions:

- Consulting others – close friends, partners or members of your family – may be a good idea.
- Set clear limits. Know what to expect per session, per day, or per week as appropriate. You may want to cut down little by little on a weekly basis.

Remember, with alcohol, there are official guidelines to 'safe' weekly limits. Keep these in mind:

- 21 units for men.
- 14 units for women.

Question whether the goal you have set for yourself is realistic. Is it do-able?

If you're in a period of abstinence, you may need to consider staying completely away from alcohol for a longer period of time. Consider whether you have failed in the past when attempting to drink in moderation. Ask yourself:

- 'Due to my alcohol use, have I experienced severe physical, mental, or social problems?'
- 'Has a doctor or other professional advised me to stop?'

If any of these factors exist, it may be an indication that you need to abstain from alcohol altogether, or it may indicate a need to ask for professional help.

Set yourself realistic goals

H45409

Planning for success

The key to reaching your goal of abstinence or drinking in moderation is planning. It's been said you should 'plan your work and work your plan.' In the case of combating alcoholism, planning for success is crucial. There are several things you should consider when making a plan.

Think about:
- Who is likely to be supportive? Is there anyone you know who has successfully stopped drinking? Could he or would he act as your mentor? Also, be aware of who you may have to avoid, such as former drinking buddies, or negative people who do not believe in your overcoming alcoholism.
- Alternative pleasures and activities that can replace your drinking. What do you enjoy best? Do you have any hobbies? Is there a pastime you've enjoyed that was replaced by your heavy drinking? Think of these activities as a reward for not drinking.
- The best time to stop – or begin cutting back – on your drinking. Is the best time next week, tomorrow . . . now? When planning to begin, be sure you stick to the time you choose – don't allow yourself to continually push it back or you may never begin the process.
- The best environment for giving up the drink or cutting down. When considering this, remember the environment should be safe and conducive to your success. If you need to avoid certain people during this time, you may need to avoid places they frequent. Depending on your personality, you may be

Alternative activities can replace your drinking

H45457

more successful in a quiet place, free from distractions. On the other hand, you may want the stimulation and distraction of activities. There is no right or wrong environment – the key to successfully reaching your goal is to do what's best for you and that it fits your personality.

One thing to remember. If a person has been professionally diagnosed as an alcoholic, he should stop drinking completely. Trying to drink moderately generally won't help. A fully-fledged alcoholic rarely succeeds in drinking in moderation. He will usually succumb to the craving and increase his consumption until he is once again abusing alcohol. On the other hand, people who have experienced alcohol-related problems may be able to successfully limit the amount they drink. However, if the person finds he cannot stay within the bounds he has set for himself, he may need to eliminate his alcohol intake completely.

A good idea when cutting down your alcohol consumption is to drink slowly. The slower you drink, the less you will drink. Also, never drink on an empty stomach. Drinking with a meal is always better. Another tip is to alternate your drinks with other, non-alcoholic, drinks. And remember, you do not need to drink when you are around other people who are drinking. If you are around people who encourage you to drink, it may be hard to decline. However, having ways to say 'no' politely will help. You may want to tell people that you feel better whenever you don't drink. If the people you hang out with still persist in your drinking and give you a hard time, it is best to stay away from them.

Another idea if you feel a desire to drink is to find something else to do such as going out to eat, going to the cinema, the theatre, or a football match. Just changing gears may help in curbing that craving and staving off that trigger. If you've ever gone on a diet – and failed – you may know somewhat of the difficulties in dealing with cravings. Most people don't eliminate forbidden foods all at once, and – as mentioned earlier – it may be easier for you to cut down rather than eliminate alcohol altogether. That's okay. And if you've set a lofty goal and do not reach it the first time, simply try again. Don't give up and don't consider yourself a failure. Surround yourself with supportive people and try, try again.

Sign that you are too drunk

You seriously believe alcohol is another food group.

If you don't achieve your goal first time, stick with it

H45816

PART 8 Revving your engine

Alcohol in and of itself is not a bad thing. Not only are there medicinal qualities, there's also fun to be had as long as it is not being abused. Drinking in moderation is key. Just as overeating may result in undesired weight gain, drinking too much may have detrimental results.

Let's consider the benefits of not drinking. What positive effects could occur if you don't drink?

• Improved physical health.
• Better mood.
• Better relations with friends and family.
• Enhanced ability to cope with life.
• Opportunities to start new hobbies or resurrect old ones.
• Development of a better self-image.

Let's consider the costs of not drinking? What negative effects could occur if you stop drinking?

• A rush of negative emotions – 'If I stop drinking, I will feel anxious, depressed, or unhappy.'
• Nothing to look forward to – feeling as if nothing will be as good or as much fun if alcohol is not involved.
• Loss of friends – 'I might lose all my friends.' 'I might be boring.' 'The relationship might change.'
• Cravings – You think you may suffer from severe alcohol cravings forever.
• Loss of social skills – 'I will be unable to function normally in social situations.'
• Unable to cope – Thinking you will lose energy, drive and confidence.

Remember when you read the passage about positive self-talk and its benefits on your road to success? Notice the above statements. Some of them show examples of negative self-talk. Negative self-talk can be as detrimental as positive self-talk is beneficial. You may be so used to this type of reinforcement that you don't realise you are doing it. However, if you become aware, you can turn your negative self-talk into positive statements. For example, rather than thinking of how miserable you will be if you stop drinking, tell yourself all the good things that will occur. Rather than thinking of losing all your friends, remind yourself of the close supportive friends you have or the supportive friendships you may form once you're alcohol-free.

You said . . . what?

It's true. Life without alcohol can be more fun than with alcohol. Look around you. Notice anything? How about those people who do not drink – the ones who just enjoy being themselves? Now, let's face it, not everyone who doesn't drink is happy or successful. There are miserable people everywhere. However, excessive alcohol consumption only compounds this game called life. Having said that, realise that life without alcohol really can be fun.

Enjoying your life for what it is

As mentioned before, people who do not drink can have fun. People who drink moderately can have fun. However, people who drink to excess, while they may be having fun times, will eventually face heartache. Observe people in a pub or nightclub who have been drinking too much – see how they think they are enjoying themselves. Those sober people around them see them as they really are. Look at how the attitudes of the sober people and those of the drinkers compare. Which group would you rather be a part of?

Take a look at children's parties. They are focused solely on food, fun and excitement. Playing games and enjoying each others' company is the key to a successful children's party. The kids love them. Now, let's look at other parties. The purpose of a party is to enjoy oneself, talk, communicate and have fun – children do this well, and completely without alcohol. If they can do it, why can't we adults? Why then do we so often feel a need for alcohol to enjoy ourselves?

Alcohol fools us. At first we think it helps us to relax and loosen up a bit. But what it does is loosen up negative feelings, insecurities and a Pandora's Box of problems. If only we could stop – break the habit – then we, like children, could learn to have real, authentic fun!

Further reading

You Can Heal Your Life. Louise L. Hay (Hay House, 1984)

Awareness. Anthony De Mello (Image; Reprint edition, 1990)

Staying Sober: A Guide for Relapse Prevention. Terence T. Gorski, Merlene Miller (Independence Press, 1986)

Photo: © iStockphoto.com, Brendon De Suza

Sex and alcohol

Photo: © iStockphoto.com, Simone van den Berg

PART 9

Effects on sexual function

In our society, as well as many others around the world, alcohol is a basic part of many of our strongest traditions, our religious rituals, such as the drinking of wine for communion, and is considered a key part of social gatherings. We raise our glass in toasting successes, and many parties feature alcohol as a way of unwinding and encouraging social interaction. Many people do not realise the implications of excessive drinking of alcohol, how strongly addictive it can be, and how, in some cases, it can literally destroy lives. In truth, alcohol is a highly addictive drug and for some people it can be a slippery road to self-destruction.

Of course, not everyone is destined to become alcohol-dependent, and most people can enjoy social drinking without negative consequences. However, for some people, certain components are already there, waiting to make drinking a real problem.

Sex and alcohol addiction

Sexual addiction is very similar in nature to other addictions and is often linked to and fuelled by alcohol. One of the most common addictions is a combination of alcohol/chemical dependency and sexual addiction.

Worst case scenario: Sexual addicts use drugs and/or alcohol to medicate themselves so as not to feel the shame of their addiction, and then become dependent on the alcohol or drugs.

How much is too much, and how does this relate to sex? No one can pinpoint the exact answer to this question since everyone responds in different ways to alcohol. The effects on any given person are linked to genetic characteristics, personality traits, body mass and other factors. One of the most common warning signs that you might have a potential problem with alcohol is the 'two drink rule.' If you find that you cannot stop drinking after two drinks and feel compelled to consume more alcohol every time you drink, this is a red flag: *you could be at risk*.

Let's talk more about sex. Most people who use alcohol feel that it mellows them, makes them feel more sexually attractive to others, and increases their sex drive. These all sound very positive, right? Who wouldn't want to feel more attractive to the opposite sex? These ideas have historically been used by advertisers to persuade us to drink alcohol.

The truth is very different. Alcohol is actually a central nervous system depressant. Its effects on sexual performance are well understood in the medical community and will be discussed further in this chapter.

> 'Health – What my friends are always drinking to before they fall down.'
> *Phyllis Diller*

Condoms are more likely to remain unused during alcohol-driven sex

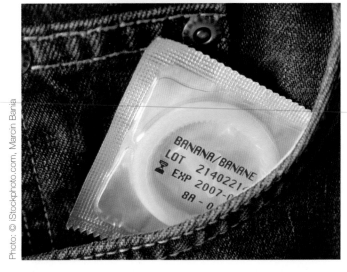

Photo: © iStockphoto.com, Marcin Bania

What's the relationship between sexual activity and alcohol use?

Of course, no one can deny that alcohol has a number of positive effects. Otherwise, so many people wouldn't enjoy using it. Alcohol tends to make us more relaxed, less inhibited, and more talkative, all things that make it easier for some people to find sexual partners. It is important, however, to remember that these positive effects of alcohol are only present at low doses, perhaps one or two units.

After three units or more, sexual activity under the influence or alcohol can become quite risky in a number of ways. Drunken sex can be messy, unsafe, uncoordinated and certainly not very erotic. There is a fine line between just enough alcohol and too much when it comes to mixing alcohol with sex.

Also, sex under the influence of alcohol is often not safe sex, as condoms or other methods of protection are much less likely to be used. Open, honest communication between partners is lessened when under the influence of any kind of drugs, alcohol included. Higher usage of alcohol can lead to forced sex with a partner who, if not actively unwilling, is at least incapable of informed consent. And this can lead to troubles with law enforcement.

The effects of alcohol on sexual function

Understanding normal sexual response and how alcohol affects you can improve your sex life.

Sex is a very complicated function, both physically and emotionally. For some people, sex is difficult, and for others it seems to just happen with no effort at all. For almost everyone, there are times when sex is great and there are also times when it's quite horrible. Sexual experiences among people are almost as varied as the people themselves in the realm of satisfaction and enjoyment.

We all understand that alcohol affects judgement. Heavy alcohol use can cause some individuals to forget that they even had sex, or to wake up naked beside a person they don't even know, and would just as soon not have to see in a sober state! Sexual arousal by itself can impair judgment, but if you add alcohol, your judgment is certain to be adversely affected. When you use alcohol, your thinking is not clear, and you may choose partners who are high-risk for disease or violence.

In addition, regular alcohol use is a contributor to impotence, as alcohol is directly toxic to the testes, causing reduced testosterone levels in men.

Although alcohol may induce desire, even moderate amounts affect the capacity to perform and respond. Dehydration from alcohol use leads to less lubrication in women, which increases the potential for painful intercourse and condom breakage, thus opening the door to the risk of unwanted pregnancy or disease. Men are less able to control sexual performance after consuming even small doses of alcohol.

Sex and alcohol facts

These symptoms are not limited to those who are alcohol-dependent, but are also found in anyone who drinks on a regular basis.

- Almost half of all of unplanned sexual encounters are under the influence of alcohol.
- More than three quarters of first sexual experiences occur under the influence of alcohol.
- Alcohol impairment often leads to: not knowing your sexual partner; not using a condom; or not using any form of contraception during sexual activity.
- In a large proportion of unplanned pregnancies, the woman was intoxicated during sex.
- More than half of all cases of sexually transmitted diseases are transmitted between sexual partners who are drunk.
- Drinking games can be used as a way for males to deliberately get females drunk quickly, for the purpose of coercing them into having sex.
- Many self-confessed date rapists said they used alcohol to get dates drunk so they would have sex.
- Many rapes and other sexual assaults occur under the influence of alcohol.
- Chronic or continuous drinking reduces testosterone output in males, and therefore, in time, can cause impotence.
- Large doses of alcohol in females may cause lack of lubrication or orgasm.
- Excessive, long-term drinking in males causes withering away of the testicles, enlargement of the breasts, loss of hair on the body, and impotence.
- Heavy drinking during pregnancy can adversely affect unborn babies (foetal alcohol syndrome).

H32855

Alcohol is directly toxic to the testes

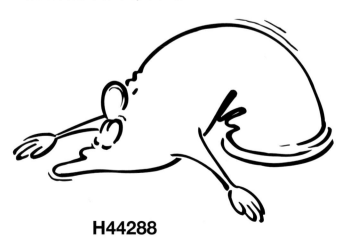

H44288

Regular alcohol use is a contributor to impotence

PART  **The good**

Alcohol is a central nervous system depressant, which means that it helps to calm us and to relax our inhibitions by depressing the actions in certain parts of the brain. Used in moderation, alcohol can help us to relax and talk more easily with others. It can also be helpful in social situations where we might be tense and need to unwind. Examples of such situations are: networking functions where we need to appear friendly and sociable, or at parties where we do not know many other people. Of course, if these situations can be managed with small amounts of alcohol, or none at all, it is obviously better.

On the other hand, we can all relate to the enjoyment of a glass of wine shared with a loved one as an introduction to sexual intimacy. This is why it is important to examine your usage of alcohol, and how it specifically affects your sexual intimacy, to determine if there are changes you should make in your lifestyle.

Drinking alcohol at social functions is not normally perceived as problematic but it is important to remember the *Sex and alcohol facts* listed in the section above to ensure that alcohol is not doing more harm than good.

Some questions to ask yourself about sex and drinking to determine how you feel about your drinking habits and whether or not you are in control:

- Have you had feelings of regret about sex the morning after because of the amount of alcohol you drank the night before?
- After an evening of drinking, have you been unable to recall events from the night before?
- Have you ever had sex with someone you would not normally choose as a sexual partner?
- Have you either made someone pregnant, or become pregnant, because of being drunk and not using condoms?
- Have you contracted a sexually transmitted disease while having sex under the influence of alcohol?
- Have you been unable to perform sexually because you were too drunk?
- Have you not enjoyed sex because you have been too drunk to connect intimately with your partner or fully respond to a sexual experience?

If you answered yes to any of these questions, it is probably a good time to consider how drinking is affecting the quality of your sex life. Don't let yourself down. Sex is a natural, joyful, healthy, and important part of life, but full enjoyment of sex requires clear thinking, responsibility in terms of pregnancy and disease, and control over our bodies in sexual situations. Too much alcohol may prevent you from making smart decisions. Sex should be good and should be enjoyed, not something which causes us shame, disease or more serious problems afterwards.

Just remember:

- Plan your evening, and the amount of alcohol you will consume.
- Know your limitation and STOP when you've reached it.
- Make your goal a positive outcome.

H34121

Full enjoyment of the sexual experience requires clear thinking

PART

The bad

It is quite common for people to use alcohol to 'loosen up.' Indeed, alcohol lowers one's inhibitions, which allows people to feel less concerned about the consequences of their activities. Studies have shown, however, that alcohol can make people do things they would not normally consider doing while sober. Alcohol also increases the chances of falling, crashing cars and becoming injured in other ways. It gives people "Dutch courage", and decreases their awareness of the risks of what they are doing. But being under the influence of alcohol is never an excuse for one's actions.

There are many dangers to be considered in using alcohol in sexual situations. The following table shows the statistics gathered by the Harvard School of Public Health on binge drinking by college students:

	Non-binge drinkers	Bingers	Frequent bingers
Did something they regretted later	14%	37%	63%
Forgot where they were or what they did	8%	26%	54%
Engaged in unplanned sexual activity	8%	20%	41%
Had unprotected sex	4%	10%	22%

Clearly, alcohol has some level of negative effect on decision-making. How can you prevent this from happening?

- Have a plan before going out for a night of drinking. Make sure you and your friends know your plans for the night. Assign a designated 'teetotaller', making sure that person is someone you can trust. If you know you do not want to have sex that night, ask your teetotaller to make sure you follow through with that decision.
- Always stay with your friends. No one can help you if you go off on your own.
- If you plan on finding a sexual partner for the evening, make sure you are prepared. Have condoms on hand.
- Try to be aware of the amount of alcohol you are consuming. Do not accept a drink prepared by someone else. Be sure what you are drinking.
- Keep watch over your glass so that your drink cannot be spiked with drugs or simply with more alcohol. Many women have had rape drugs slipped into their drink. If you glance away for a split second this can happen, so be careful and alert.

Social gatherings or parties are a great place to meet new people, relax, and have fun safely. However, at their worst, they can become the source of alcohol poisoning, or sexual assault. Any amount of alcohol can lead to impaired judgement, which in turn can have dangerous consequences. The steps outlined above are a good way to increase your level of safety and help make your memories good ones.

Blackouts

When you can't remember all or part of what occurred during the time you were drinking, even though you appeared to be acting normally to others, you have had a blackout. Blackouts occur when the amount of alcohol you have consumed overtakes your brain's normal ability to properly process information.

Blackouts are dangerous for many reasons. Most importantly, if you don't remember what you did, you may have engaged in risky behaviours such as unprotected or unplanned sexual activity or driving under the influence. If is also possible for an individual to be a victim of a crime, such as rape, during a blackout, with no knowledge of this having occurred. Frequent blackouts are a warning sign of problem drinking.

Sexually Transmitted Infections (STIs)

Learning the basics of sex

No! This is not the ABC of sex! This area deals with STIs (sexually transmitted infections) and the reasons why having sex whilst one is under the influence of alcohol can be a health hazard. STIs make up more than 20 different infections that can be transmitted through the exchange of semen, blood, and other body fluids, or by direct contact with the affected body areas of infected people. You probably know how to enjoy sex, but to have a safe sexual experience, it is important to always use a condom to guard against most STIs.

H44297

Correct use of a condom is difficult under the influence of alcohol

When drinking, people often forget to use condoms or are so 'out of it' that they cannot make good decisions regarding safe sex. For a condom to work, it has to be put on correctly. No problem, you say? But if you have been drinking heavily, and can barely walk or see without covering one of your eyes, it's not likely that you will be able to put on a condom correctly.

Various studies have proven that people who get drunk on a regular basis are less likely to use condoms. In addition, inconsistently using condoms or using them incorrectly during sexual activity increases the risk of getting sexually transmitted diseases. Some STIs can be treated and cured. Herpes, genital warts and HIV/AIDS are incurable – they will be with you for as long as you live.

People with alcohol dependency are a high risk group for STIs. Alcohol lowers a person's inhibitions, therefore leading to the likelihood of risky sexual behaviour.

The Center for Disease Control and Prevention in the US has reported that 85% of the most prevalent infectious diseases in the United States are sexually transmitted. The rate of STIs in many westernised countries is growing at an alarming rate. As many as one in four sexually active people in will be affected by an STI at some time in his or her life. Pretty scary!

Types of STIs

STIs can have very painful and life-long consequences, in addition to immediate health problems. They can cause:

- Birth defects.
- Blindness.
- Bone deformities.
- Brain damage.
- Cancer.
- Heart disease.
- Infertility and other abnormalities of the reproductive system.
- Mental retardation.
- Death.

Some of the most common and potentially serious STIs include:

- Chlamydial diseases – including lymphogranuloma venereum (LGV) and chlamydial urethritis – and gonorrhoea. These STIs can cause sterility or potentially fatal infections of the upper genital tract. Women may not know they have this disease until they have been rendered sterile.
- Human Papilloma Virus (HPV) – HPV causes genital warts in both sexes. It is the single most important risk factor for cervical cancer in women. Removal of the warts can be painful, and is only a temporary measure anyway, since the virus remains in the body and the warts can come back.
- Genital Herpes – Herpes is an incurable viral infection thought to be one of the most common STIs in the UK.
- Syphilis – Syphilis can be a potentially life-threatening infection which also increases the chances of acquiring or transmitting HIV.
- Human Immunodeficiency Virus (HIV) infection – There is no cure for this STI, although new combination medications have been developed which can defer the onset of full-blown AIDS, or at least extend the life of those who have contracted this disease.

What if you think you have an STI?

A sexually active person who has symptoms of an STI or who has had sexual contact with another person known to have an STI should consult a GP or attend the local genitourinary medicine (GUM) or STI clinic.

Diagnosis begins with a physical examination and medical history that documents the patient's sexual history and assesses the risk of infection.

The doctor or other healthcare professional will:

- Describe the testing process needed.
- Explain the meaning of the test results when received.
- Provide the patient with information regarding high-risk behaviours.
- Provide any necessary treatments or procedures.

Many doctors suggest that a patient who has been diagnosed with one STI be tested for others. It is entirely possible to have more than one STI at a time, since one infection may create a climate that allows for the growth of others. It is very important that persons who are HIV-positive be tested for syphilis as well.

If you think you might have an STI, consult the professionals without delay

H39916

PART 9 The ugly

The less attractive aspects of sex and alcohol are its role in:

- Sexual behaviour.
- Sexual aggression.
- Unwanted sex.
- Lack of inhibition.
- Using intoxication as an excuse for rape and violence.

Sexual aggression, domestic and other violence, and rape are often attributed to the abuse of alcohol. Alcohol cannot make a man abuse a woman, but it is frequently used as an excuse when this behaviour occurs. There are many men who drink and do not abuse anyone. Many men abuse women when they are sober. Perhaps it is easier for some men and women to accept that the violence would not have occurred if alcohol had not been involved.

Alcoholism and battering do share similar characteristics – both may be passed from generation to generation, through environmentally-learned behaviour. Both involve denial of the problem, and both involve isolation of the family affected.

However, there is no research evidence that alcohol abuse *causes* domestic violence.

Rape

Numerous research studies have shown that alcohol plays a role in at least 70% of date rape cases. It is important to note that alcohol is involved in sexual assaults at least ten times more often than other date rape drugs. The drug cases are most often reported by the media in connection with rape, while alcohol-related rapes are not as likely to draw media attention.

Rape occurs when one person forces another to do something sexual against that person's will. Rape is a crime.

Remember that:

- Any person has the right to say no to sex for any reason.
- Rape is never the victim's fault. No one 'asks' to be raped.
- Date or acquaintance rape is allegedly very prevalent but often goes unreported.
- In addition to men raping women: women can rape women, men can rape men and women can rape men.

Being under the influence of alcohol is never an excuse for forcing sex on an unwilling person. If the victim of the assault is too drunk to give informed consent, it's still rape, and still a crime. If the rapist is too drunk to know what he or she is doing, it's still rape, and still a crime.

No means no. Yes while drunk can also mean no.

Preventing rape

The largest proportion of rapes are 'date rapes'. You can reduce your chances of being a victim of date rape by remembering the following:

- When going out with someone new, you do not have to go alone. Suggest going on a group date or agree to meet in a public place.
- Choose new dates who socialise with people who have the same values and beliefs as you.
- Communicate honestly with your date. Don't send mixed signals or flirt aggressively, even with someone you know, if you don't intend to have sex with them.
- Be aware on dates. Have open options on what you will do, pay your own way; make sure you have your own transport if needed.
- Take care of yourself. Don't put yourself in a situation where you might be alone with someone you do not know well. Be sure that you know where you are going, and that other people will be present.
- Be very cautious about going into someone else's home or inviting them into yours. These locations are the places where most date rapes occur.
- Listen to and trust your instincts. If you don't feel comfortable – leave.

If despite your precautions, things start to get out of hand, leave if possible, or protest firmly and loudly. Don't be afraid to call for help if necessary.

Finally, don't date anyone who abuses alcohol.

Legal issues

Violence and alcohol seem to go hand in hand. Although a relationship between alcohol and violence exists, it is not entirely understood. Alcohol itself does not seem to cause aggression. It's extremely unlikely that alcohol will cause a well-adjusted person to spontaneously start punching another person for no reason. However, in someone who is already aggressive, alcohol does seem to increase the chance that they will act on aggressive urges. Also, alcohol has been shown to increase the chance that a non-aggressive person may react aggressively if provoked.

It has been found that it is typically what people think rather than what they drink that is important after drinking heavily. This is to say that it is not likely that you are a Dr. Jekyll and Mr. Hyde, with alcohol being the secret elixir that may cause you to become violent. However, if you are suffering from deep-seated feelings of loss, sadness, anger or aggression, or have existing problems in a relationship, excessive consumption of alcohol could release the normal, healthy, inhibitions that are keeping you from acting out aggressively.

Therefore, it is possible that inappropriate sexual behaviour and aggression may be more a result of what we believe than of the amount of alcohol we actually consume.

For the most part, it is our culture and belief system that allow for the connection between sex, alcohol and violence. Some people use this belief to justify their behaviours and to avoid personal responsibility. However, the bottom line is: alcohol is NOT an excuse for unacceptable behaviour of any kind.

PART 9

Yeah baby!

Having fun with alcohol and sex

Sex is a wonderful and certainly a very important part of life, but the fullest enjoyment of sexuality requires us to be clear thinking, responsible and in control. Being under the influence of too much alcohol will prevent us from making the best decisions, and having the best sex!

Health experts around the world agree that small amounts of alcohol, especially red wine, can be good for you. In moderate amounts it can reduce sexual inhibitions, intensify our libido and temporarily enhance self-esteem. Wine and romance are so closely associated that we tend to think of dinner and a glass of wine as a romantic evening.

> Drinking alcohol may very well be the leading cause of pregnancy.

Photo: © iStockphoto.com, Sandra O'Claire

A guy spots a nice looking girl in a bar goes up and starts small talk. Seeing that she didn't back off he asked her name.

'Carmen,' she replied.

That's a nice name,' he said warming up the conversation. 'Who named you, your mother?'

'No, I named myself,' she answered.

'Oh, that's interesting. Why Carmen?'

'Because I like cars, and I like men,' she said looking directly into his eyes. 'So what's your name?' she asked.

'Beersex.'

> 'One reason I don't drink is that I want to know when I'm having a good time.'
> Lady Astor

Do alcohol and sex make lousy lovers?

As Shakespeare said 'It provokes the desire, but it takes away the performance.' Heavy drinking can dull sensation and make it more difficult for men to have an erection and for woman to reach orgasm. This is a good reason to make sure your drinking is controlled in sexual situations.

Alcohol and sexuality do tend to mix well. Alcohol is widely regarded around the world as a very effective formula for loosening sexual inhibitions. Our cultural images of alcohol and sexuality combined as one are quite commonplace. Some examples are: champagne on the wedding night, wine with a romantic dinner, tropical drinks being enjoyed by bikini-clad women, and student parties. Our culture is filled with this type of alcohol/sexuality imagery.

The message, especially in advertising, seems to suggest that alcohol and sexuality are interchangeable themes. The subliminal message is that alcohol can enhance sexual activities. But can alcohol truly generate these magical effects? Perhaps alcohol merely serves as scapegoat for the possibilities we do not normally see for ourselves.

Using alcohol to relax sexual inhibitions and to enhance romantic and sexual feelings is not typically a problem. It is more of a pleasure. However, as previously noted, alcohol has also been implicated in many unpleasant and serious outcomes, including unwanted pregnancy, sexual dysfunction, sexual assault, and sexually transmitted infections (including HIV/AIDS). Thus, it seems that alcohol has ties with a variety of sexual outcomes.

The key to a safe and satisfying sexual encounter is to keep your alcohol consumption under control. It will be more gratifying for both you and your partner.

Using alcohol safely

PART 10 **Party time**

Everyone loves a good party. While you can have a good party with or without alcohol, the key to having fun with alcohol is to know your limitations. Whether you are at a party, a family gathering, or out with a few friends, drinking in moderation may mean the difference between having a good time and winding up in the gutter.

We've all heard the statistics around the holiday season when parties are in full bloom. It is the worst time of the year for drinking and driving accidents. Even if you aren't drinking, you have to assume that others are, so you must always be aware of whom you ride with as well as the other vehicles on the road. It is wise to designate a sober driver and to carry enough money in your pocket in case you need to call a taxi. Also, if you feel a need to have a glass in your hand just to fit in with the crowd, remember you can order a 'virgin' drink.

When hosting a party, you are in charge. Offering both alcoholic and non-alcoholic drinks is considerate to your guests, plus you can limit your own alcohol intake while still drinking throughout the evening. Moderation is the key to having fun safely with alcohol.

Over the page are a few simple recipes from www.bbc.co.uk/threecounties/content/articles/2005/01/04/think_drink_cocktails_feature.shtml that can be as delicious as any alcoholic beverage.

Sign you are too drunk
Biting you makes a mosquito stagger.

Everyone loves a good party

H45818

San Francisco

Serves 1
Treat your taste buds!

3 ice cubes
1 measure orange juice
1 measure lemon juice
1 measure pineapple juice
1 measure grapefruit juice
2 dashes grenadine
1 egg white
soda water

Put the ice cubes into a cocktail shaker and pour in the orange, lemon, pineapple and grapefruit juices, grenadine and egg white. Shake well then strain into a large goblet. Top up with soda water and decorate with the lemon and lime slices, a cocktail cherry on a cocktail stick and an orange spiral. Serve with a straw.

To decorate:
Lemon slice, Lime slice, Cocktail cherry, Orange spiral

Bugs Bunny

Serves 1

50 ml (2fl oz) carrot juice
50 ml (2fl oz) orange juice
4-6 ice cubes
1 dash Tabasco sauce
1 celery stick, to decorate

Pour the carrot and orange juices into a tumbler over ice, add a dash of Tabasco and decorate with a celery stick.

Romanov Fizz

Serves 2

8-10 ripe strawberries, hulled
125 ml (4 fl oz) orange juice
2 ice cubes
125 ml (4 fl oz) soda water

Put the strawberries and orange juice into a food processor and process until smooth. Place 1 ice cube in each of 2 sour glasses or wine glasses and add the strawberry liquid. Pour the soda water into the food processor, process briefly and use to top up the glasses. Stir briskly, and serve.

Photo: © iStockphoto.com, Gustaf Brundin

Photo: © iStockphoto.com, Rebecca Ellis

Photo: © iStockphoto.com, Nina Shannon

Appleade

Serves 3

2 large dessert apples
600 m (1 pint) boiling water
½ teaspoon sugar
ice cubes
apple slices, to decorate

Chop the apples and place in a bowl. Pour the boiling water over the apples and add the sugar. Leave to stand for 1-2 minutes, then strain into a jug and allow to cool. Pour over ice cubes in tall glasses and decorate with apple slices. Serve with straws.

Photo: © iStockphoto.com, Heiko Bennewitz

Chocolate Shake

Serves 1

2 measures chocolate syrup
2 scoops chocolate ice cream
1 scoop vanilla ice cream
250 ml (8 fl oz) full-fat milk
whipped cream, to decorate (optional)

Pour all of the ingredients into a food processor. Process well until the desired thickness is reached. Pour into a tall glass. Decorate with whipped cream, if liked, and serve with straw.

Photo: © iStockphoto.com, Kasia Biel

Keep Sober

Serves 1

½ measure grenadine
½ measure lemon syrup
3 measures tonic water
soda water
ice cubes

Put the grenadine, lemon syrup and tonic water in a tumbler and stir together. Top up with soda water and add ice cubes, if liked.

Photo: © iStockphoto.com, Ivan Mateev

Variation
For a tangier drink, replace the grenadine with lime syrup and decorate the drink with lime slices.

PART 10 When enough is enough

There comes a time when you must realise that enough is enough. All people are different and are affected differently by alcohol. Some can have two drinks and still be in control while others should not have even that much. The key to drinking and staying in control is to know your limits . . . and stick to them.

> A hangover is the wrath of grapes.
> Anonymous

Once a drinker finds that point where he has had enough, he can begin to control his drinking and set a goal to that end. Obviously, if the drinker received a great amount of social support and had few negative influences, he would have a better chance of maintaining a goal of controlled drinking without relapse. Gender, in relation to the other two factors, does not make much of a difference in this case. However, because of the differences in height and build, women are more susceptible to the quicker onset of liver disease.

Can I do it?

Sure, you can! People recover from alcohol-dependency every day, as well as other addictions, such as drugs, overeating, gambling, and co-dependency. However, rarely does someone overcome his addictions alone. A support network is key to reaching and maintaining your goal, whether your goal is abstinence or drinking in moderation (controlled drinking). You can get sober and stay sober. It's do-able.

> 'Time is never wasted when you're wasted all the time.' If this quote by Catherine Zandonella describes you, you may not know when enough is enough.

Frequently asked questions

Why do people use alcohol?
* People use substances such as alcohol because they like the way it makes them feel. Pleasure is an all-consuming force. All drugs that are addicting, including alcohol, can activate and affect the brain's pleasure circuitry. Our brains are wired in such a way that if we do something that gives us pleasure we tend to want to do it again.

What is an alcohol addiction?
* This is a disease that affects your brain. It also affects your behaviour. Once you become addicted to alcohol, you drink without thinking of the consequences, such as health problems, money problems, relationship problems, and poor performance at work.

Can I know if I have a problem?
* Yes, you have a problem with alcohol if you continue to drink even when it causes problems with your health, money, work, or with your personal relationships. You have a problem if you have developed a tolerance to alcohol. Remember, this means you need to use more to get the desired effect.

Can I be treated for alcohol addiction?
* Yes, but remember, addiction is a disease. It is chronic, which means it can go on for a long time. It may take a several attempts to stay free of alcohol or to maintain a goal of controlled drinking.

What kinds of treatments are available?
* You should consult your GP for treatments he recommends for you. Some treatments may include counselling while others include medication.

How can I stop or cut down on alcohol?
* First, understand that you are in charge of your actions. You are in charge of your positive self-talk. You are in control of your choice to drink or not to drink. Ultimately, that is the question.

> You don't have to drink to play darts – but it helps!
> *Anonymous*

Is controlled/moderate drinking OK for me?

This is a question you should ask your GP before deciding to continue drinking, even moderately. In some cases, it's not just heavy drinkers that are at risk for damaging their health. Every person is different. There are several factors to consider when determining if you can drink moderately and get by with it without damaging your liver. These factors include:

- Age.
- Genetic make-up.
- Body build.
- Gender.
- Ethnicity.

If a person is susceptible to liver disease, too much alcohol for him may seem like a small amount for someone else. In order to make sure your alcohol consumption – however large or small – is right for you, be sure to talk it over with your doctor. One of the reasons you're cutting down on alcohol is to take charge of your life and make it better. Be sure what you're doing has positive consequences and not negative ones.

For some people, even one unit of alcohol a day is too many. However, once a person is drinking more than six units per day, his risk hits a plateau. Generally, the later in life a person begins to drink, the better. Young livers are more vulnerable to alcohol damage than those in older people. The increase in alcoholic liver disease can often be attributed to heavy drinking in younger people.

In addition to alcohol, there are several other factors that can cause cirrhosis or other liver diseases, regardless of alcohol consumption:

- Obesity.
- Medications.
- Herbal remedies.
- Illegal drugs.
- Exposure to certain chemicals.
- The presence of Hepatitis C.

If you find that you fall into one or more of the above categories, your chances of damaging your liver with alcohol consumption are compounded. Periodic liver function blood tests are crucial to monitor possible trouble around the bend.

Is it all bad news?

Thankfully, no. There are some advantages to consuming alcohol. Yes, you read that right. In diabetic patients, a drink may reduce the probability of a heart attack by 75% for men and 61% for women. However, be aware that consuming large quantities of alcohol on an empty stomach is a no-no. Always accompany your drinking with food whenever possible, or – and this is the best advice – don't drink alcohol at all when you're not eating.

Another perk is alcohol's effect on cardiovascular patients. In these patients – with men over 40 years of age and in post-menopausal women – protective elements are relevant if alcohol is consumed in moderation. Yes, we are back to controlled drinking.

Coming of age

Suppose you're a student at university. You and your buddies go out for drinks quite frequently. You're young and invincible – or so you think. Is it really that important to regulate your alcohol consumption when you're young? Really?

Take a look at the following myths young people commonly believe to be true:

No matter how much I drink, I'm still in control
Myth buster: Drinking does impair your judgment, even when you're not aware of it. Because of this, it increases the likelihood that you will do something you'll regret later. These 'somethings' may be participating in unprotected sex, date rape, or vandalism.

My driving is not affected after a few drinks
Myth buster: Believe it or not, about half of all fatal vehicle crashes among 18 to 24 year olds involve alcohol.

Spirits have more alcohol than beer
Myth buster: A standard measure of 40% ABV spirits, or 125ml of wine, has roughly the same amount of alcohol as half a pint of beer.

I just need to learn to 'hold my booze'
Myth buster: Usually a person considers he has learnt to 'hold his booze' when it becomes necessary for him to drink more alcohol to get the same 'buzz' he used to experience with less. This is a sign of developing a tolerance to alcohol. Tolerance is a warning sign of possibly developing more serious problems with alcohol.

I'm just drinking to keep up with my boyfriend
Myth buster: It's a known fact that women process alcohol differently. No matter how much your male friend drinks, if you – as a woman – drink the same amount, you will be more intoxicated and impaired than him.

I can drink as much as I want and then sober up quickly
Myth buster: Contrary to popular opinion, nothing speeds up the process of sobriety, not even cold showers or coffee. Two units of alcohol generally take two to three hours to eliminate.

Drinking alcohol isn't all that dangerous; I can drink and be okay
Myth buster: Unfortunately, this is not true. One-third of 18 to 24 year olds admitted to hospitals for serious injuries are drunk. Not only this, but many drownings, murders and suicides are associated with alcohol consumption.

Drinking and driving don't mix

Photo: © iStockphoto.com, Jim Jurica

PART **10** # Some can, some can't

It's true. Some people who have been heavy drinkers can set a goal of moderation – or controlled drinking – and actually stick with it. Others find that no matter what goals they set, they can never reach them. For those folks, a goal of abstinence may be in order.

> When the wine is in, the wit is out.
> *Proverb*

Anyone who abuses alcohol will find it helpful to set goals to cut back their alcohol consumption. Those who are alcohol-dependent are in a whole different ball game. For them, abstinence is most likely the only way to enjoy a successful life.

What is alcohol-dependence? And how do I know if I'm alcohol-dependent?

Alcohol-dependence is a disease. To find out if you are alcohol-dependent, check to see if you exhibit the following symptoms:

- **Craving** – This is a strong urge to have a drink, so strong that you feel you 'need' a drink.
- **Dependence** – This is a physical dependence, characterised by withdrawal symptoms such as the shakes, excessive sweating, nausea, and feelings of anxiety when you have stopped drinking.
- **Lack of control** – This is when you feel you cannot stop drinking once you've begun. You aren't in charge of the amount of alcohol you are consuming.
- **Tolerance** – This goes back to your need, only instead of a craving, this is a need to get the 'high' you experienced before on a lesser amount of alcohol.

The craving caused by alcohol-dependency can be as strong as the cravings we all experience for food and water. Despite serious consequences, the drinker will do almost anything to get a drink. It is a hard habit to break, even when he sees the devastating effects alcohol is having on his life, family, health, work and social relationships.

Classified as a disease, alcohol-dependency has its own symptoms, just like any other disease. It is also chronic, which means that it lasts throughout the person's lifetime. Many believe that the risk for developing an alcohol-dependency is heavily dependent on a person's inherited genes and also his lifestyle. Research has determined that risk for alcohol-dependency is found in members of the same family. While this points to a genetic factor, it may also point to a lifestyle factor.

Obviously, we are all influenced in some degree by the environment we are raised in and live in. Our families, friends, co-workers, and the amount of stress in our lives may promote the risk. However, even if you have many risk factors toward alcohol-dependency, that does not mean you will become alcohol-dependent or that you can't overcome it.

You are in control of your life. Your destiny is not predetermined by genetic or environmental factors, although they weigh in heavily.

Sure, alcohol-dependency runs in families. That's a fact. But that does not necessarily mean that children from those families have no hope. Some people whose family members do not exhibit drinking problems will develop problems with alcohol. On the other hand, some people never develop problems with alcohol although they come from families with drinking problems. Still, it is good to know your risk factors so you can arm yourself with that knowledge and then take appropriate steps against developing problems with alcohol.

Unfortunately, though alcohol-dependency is a disease, it cannot be cured. Suffering a relapse is a risk even when the person has not been drinking for a long time. This is true for those who have an alcohol-dependency, not just a heavy drinker who needs to cut down. A person dependent on alcohol, who has this disease, must guard against falling prey to alcohol cravings. He must avoid alcohol at all costs in order not to suffer a relapse. Moderate or controlled drinking is not an option for him. With treatment, the drinker can overcome his addiction and rebuild his life.

Different people require different treatments. During the first few days after an alcohol-dependent person stops drinking, he will need prescription drugs to help him safely withdraw. The drugs, typically benzodiazepines, are only used for a short time because they are highly addictive. Other drugs can help a person from relapsing into heavy drinking. The drug disulfiram will actually make a person feel sick if he drinks alcohol, thereby discouraging its use.

These drugs, while good, are in no way miracle cures. Each person is different and will respond differently. Even today, researchers continue to find more effective medications to treat alcohol-dependency.

Some drugs will make a person feel sick and discourage alcohol use

H44298

Treatment for alcohol-dependency can be beneficial. Without it, many people would never wean themselves away from the bottle . . . the wine bottle, that is. Even with treatment, some still have a hard time in remaining abstinent. And as with any chronic disease, there are different levels of success when it comes to treatment. Some completely quit drinking and stay sober for the rest of their lives. Others have long periods of sobriety, with lapses of drinking in between. Others find they just cannot resist the craving of alcohol for any good length of time. However, one thing is certain: the longer a person does not drink alcohol, the greater his chances are of being able to stay sober.

Now, having said that, let's look at the difference between alcohol-dependency – which is what we have been referring to – and alcohol abuse. There is a difference. A person can abuse alcohol and yet not be dependent upon it. Anytime a person drinks to excess he has abused alcohol. Again, moderation or controlled drinking is preferable. Now, it's pretty easy to spot alcohol-dependence for the problems are severe and far-reaching. However, how do you know if you are an alcohol abuser? Take a quick assessment and see if any of these problems belong to you:

• Unable to work.
• Unable to meet deadlines.
• Unable to function at school.
• Unable to meet family responsibilities.
• Involvement in vehicle accidents.
• Having been arrested for drunk driving.
• Experiencing adverse medical conditions related to drinking alcohol.

Think about it. If you experience any of the above problems, you may be abusing alcohol. If so, it's time to take an evaluation and decide what you are going to do about it. In addition to the above criteria, there are a few other circumstances that warrant the term 'alcohol abuse.' These do not necessarily include heavy drinking, but even moderate drinking may be a culprit if you combine it with pregnancy, driving, or when taking certain medications.

Drinking during pregnancy is dangerous because alcohol can have a number of harmful effects on the baby. It can be born mentally retarded or with learning and behavioural problems. No one knows exactly how much alcohol is required to cause these problems. However, these alcohol-related birth defects are entirely preventable, simply by not drinking alcohol during pregnancy. The safest course for women who are pregnant or trying to become pregnant is to drink no alcohol at all – none, nada, zilch.

By the way, alcohol abuse and alcohol-dependency both can affect anyone, with no respect to race, gender, or nationality. However, it has been noted that people who begin drinking at an early age – say, in their early teens or younger – greatly increase their risk of becoming alcohol-dependent. Remember when you read about 'tolerance'? People who begin drinking early will experience that 'tolerance' to alcohol, therefore consuming more of it to get the same desired effect. If that continues, they may become alcohol-dependent as their consumption has not only increased, but their cravings become more intense as well.

What to do if you suspect you have a drinking problem?

First, ask yourself the following questions:

- Do you become annoyed when people criticise your drinking?
- Does your drinking make you feel guilty?
- Have you ever thought that you should cut back on the amount of alcohol you consume?
- Do you ever feel a need to have a drink first thing in the morning to calm your nerves?

If you answered 'yes' to at least one of those questions, be aware. You may have an alcohol problem. If you answered 'yes' to more than one, it is highly likely that you have an alcohol problem. Your best bet would be to see your GP and find out if a real drinking problem exists. If so, you – along with your doctor – can then plan the best course of action for you. Now, if you find you are alcohol-dependent, you will need to abstain from alcohol completely, as alcohol-dependency is a disease. However, if you find you are experiencing alcohol-related problems, you may be able to eliminate those problems by cutting back or controlling your drinking. Even so, if you try to cut back and find that you are consistently going over your limits, you may need to stop drinking altogether.

Now, let's say that you are not the one with the drinking problem. Let's say it is someone close to you. Someone you want to help. And not just someone you want to help, but someone that is unwilling to accept help or get help. What can you do? A situation like this is definitely a challenge. If the person is alcohol-dependent, it may be that an incident occurs to warrant court-ordered treatment or a medical emergency. Hopefully, this will not be the case. The way you can help is to stop covering up for the drinker. This is often a natural action. You don't want to be embarrassed by their drinking and you don't want them to be embarrassed. You make excuses in order to 'protect' the drinker. However, if you continue to cover up his drinking, he will never have to face the consequences of it. If he doesn't face the consequences, he will never stop – there is no reason to.

Once you stop the cover up, you need to confront the drinker about his problem. This will not be easy and he will probably become quite defensive. That is a natural reaction to being challenged, especially if the person being challenged is in the wrong and doesn't want to admit it.

For best results, pick the best time to talk. For a drinker, the best time is shortly after a problem – alcohol-related – has occurred; while it is fresh in his mind, while you have something you can point to in proving your point that alcohol has become a problem for him. Sometimes this is a serious argument within the family unit, a vehicle accident, or a negative situation at work.

Make sure the drinker is sober when you talk to him and also that he is fairly calm. He will be more receptive to you if he is. Also, it is imperative that you speak to him in private. When you speak to him, be specific. Tell him you are worried about his excessive drinking and how it is affecting him. Point out – not in an accusatory way – some of the problems that have been caused by his drinking, being sure to mention the most current incident. Make sure he is aware of the problems his drinking is causing you as well.

Be honest. Tell him what you will do if he does not choose to go for help. You may need to refuse to go with him to any social events where you know he will drink. Or you may need to act more drastically, telling him you are moving out of the house if he does not go for help. However, do not say this unless you are prepared to follow through. If he calls your bluff and you do not follow through, he will realise it is an empty threat and your words will not carry any weight.

The next step is to get help. If the drinker is willing to go for help, do not wait for him to change his mind. Call and get an appointment with his GP or at some other treatment centre. You should offer to go with him as this is not only an important step, but may also be a bit scary for the drinker.

Let's say – worst case scenario – you've spoken to the drinker in private, when he is sober and calm, and he refuses to seek help. Now would be a good time to call on a concerned friend or family member. Talk with them first, letting them know how to approach the drinker and how you've talked to him and his reaction. Any person who is caring may help. However, if you know someone who has recovered from alcohol-dependency, his words may carry more weight with the drinker. Sometimes it takes more than one approach to convince the drinker that he really needs to seek help. At times it may be necessary to join with other family members and/or friends and confront the drinker. However, before doing so, it's best to get the guidance of a professional.

No matter what action the drinker takes or does not take, it is important that you get the help you need. Those affected by another's alcohol problem can seek out support from groups located in most communities. These groups will help you to understand and accept the fact that you are not responsible – no matter how you may feel – for the drinker's abuse of alcohol or even whether he chooses to get help for himself. Support groups will also help you to realise you need to take care of yourself.

The female factor

When ingested by a woman, alcohol causes her to be more impaired than a man who drinks the same amount of alcohol, even when body weight differences are taken into account. Why? Women's bodies have less water than men's. Therefore, the alcohol a woman ingests will be more concentrated. That is one reason that the recommended drinking limit for women is lower than for men. Once a woman begins abusing alcohol repeatedly, she will experience physical problems more rapidly than a man. These can range from liver damage to problems with her brain and heart.

Women are more affected by alcohol than men

So what's a girl to do?

Fortunately, there is good news. According to independent studies, moderate – or controlled – drinkers are less likely to die from heart disease compared with people who do not drink at all or are heavy drinkers. Interesting, isn't it? Moderate for a woman would most likely be two units or less per day.

The male review

While alcohol is not as potent for men as for women, there is still cause for concern. Moderate drinking, or controlled drinking, would be three units or less per day. If you're drinking more than

Alcohol may be good for the heart, but there are better ways to keep it healthy

Be wary of strong drink – it can make you shoot at tax collectors . . . and miss.
Robert Heinlein

that, you may be at risk for alcohol abuse. Cutting back would be a good idea. However, research has shown that a man drinking two units per day is less likely to die from heart disease than is his non-drinking or heavy-drinking counterpart. It's possible that small amounts of alcohol reduce the risk of blood clots by changing the blood's chemistry.

Having said that, if you do not currently drink alcohol, this is not a good reason to start. There are other – better – ways to keep your heart in tip-top shape. Eating nutritional foods and exercising are good ways to stay heart healthy. Keep in mind that heavy drinking actually increases the risk of stroke, high blood pressure, cirrhosis and heart failure.

What happens as we age? Is it better to drink if you're older?

Not really – at least not to excess. As people age, their reaction time is slower, they have problems with their hearing and vision, and they have a lower tolerance for alcohol. When you combine that with alcohol's effects, the combination can be deadly. Older people who drink alcohol – and especially those who are alcohol-dependent – are at a greater risk for falls, vehicle accidents, and other alcohol-related injuries. Also, older people generally take more prescription drugs than younger people. Many drugs have labels that warn alcohol should not be consumed when taking them. Doing so is dangerous and may be fatal.

Alcohol consumption in older people can also worsen medical conditions such as high blood pressure and ulcers. A good plan would be (if you're older) to limit yourself to one unit per day, provided you're not taking any drugs which warn against alcohol consumption.

Just what is controlled drinking?

Both abstinence and drinking in moderation have been mentioned in this manual. By now you may have decided which pathway is right for you. The choice isn't always easy, but it will be worthwhile. Whether you have chosen to drink in moderation or to abstain completely, your first step toward reaching your goal will most likely be the same.

Most people find it easier to commit to abstinence if they do it little by little, rather than giving up their friend the bottle all at once. Some healthcare providers in both the UK and the US recommend abstinence for higher-severity problem drinkers. If you fall into that category, chances are, abstinence is your best bet for a full recovery from your alcohol dependence. Controlled drinking seems to be recommended more often in the UK than the US with the recommendation varying according to the drinker's characteristics and their country.

Controlled drinking consists of limiting how much and how often you drink. Basically, it is drinking in moderation. Doing this will eliminate – or at least lessen – the negative consequences related to your drinking. To control your drinking, you may need professional help or you may be able to do it on your own. The severity of alcohol-dependence is key to knowing whether or not professional help is needed.

No matter how you arrive at your goal, you will feel a deep satisfaction when you succeed. And your success will not only affect you, but the lives of those around you – family, friends, and co-workers. The positive effects of controlling your drinking may be mirrored in your work environment, your social life, and your family environment. You may be surprised at how good life can be when your craving for alcohol does not control you.

There are several factors to consider when determining if controlled drinking is a realistic goal for you.

- Environmental factors – Where do you hang out? Are the places you frequent conducive to drinking or abstinence?
- Relationships – Who do you associate with? Are they supportive in your efforts to cut back or drinking or do they encourage drinking?
- Psychological factors – What is your mindset concerning your drinking? Do you believe in yourself and your abilities? Is a fear of failure holding you back? Are you using positive self talk to help reach your goal?

Worldwide, controlled drinking is supported mostly in the UK, but also in New South Wales, Norway, and Australia. The US tends to promote abstinence rather than controlled drinking in their treatment programmes. These programmes include halfway houses and inpatient detoxification and rehabilitation services. In the case of outpatient programmes, the US was more lenient in encouraging controlled drinking, though still just for a minority of their clientele. Canadian alcohol treatment agencies fall somewhere in the middle.

When assessing whether people were good candidates for controlled drinking rather than abstinence, several factors were considered:

- The severity of negative influences of the drinker's alcohol consumption.
- The level of family/social support the drinker received.
- The gender of the drinker.

For you, personally, it's imperative that you know if you can drink or if you can't. And if you can, how much can you drink and still be in control? It may be helpful to consider your typical day. Think about it, from beginning to end. Consider your thoughts and actions from the time your feet hit the floor in the morning until you close your eyes in sleep at night. Now ask yourself, 'In my typical day, how does alcohol fit in?'

Once you've answered that question honestly, you will have a good idea whether or not you have an alcohol problem. Once you assess the extent that alcohol may be causing problems in your life – be it through your health, family, work, or social relationships – you can begin to take steps to cut back or cut out alcohol in your life.

Yes, there are ways to have fun while maintaining control of your alcohol intake. The best way is to first make the choice to do what's best for you and your health to combat the negative effects alcohol may be having on your life and the lives of those around you. It's true that not everyone can drink alcohol. You may be one of the ones that need to remain abstinent. If that's the case, don't be discouraged. There are many like you. Just remember that alcohol itself is not your key to living a happy and successful life. Once you've got your alcohol consumption under control, live life to the fullest – and enjoy!

Kids and alcohol don't mix

Photo: © iStockphoto.com, Kenn Wislander

PART  A deadly combination

Emotions rise high in the teenage years causing a rift between teens and their parents. This can get even worse if the teen begins drinking alcohol. Adolescence can be a tough time for all, mainly because of the rapid physical changes and high emotional states. While it can be an exciting time for the teenager, it can also be confusing. Not just for the teen but his parents as well. The following information may help you as you figure out how to approach your teen about alcohol consumption and how to deal with your teen if you suspect he is drinking. You'll also learn about the process your teen goes through as he enters adolescence and some of the problems that can cause.

Difficult as it might be, if you suspect your child is drinking you have to do something . . .

Photos: © iStockphoto.com, Timothy Large

. . . the same goes for smoking

Youngsters look to adults for guidance

Children and alcohol are a dangerous and sometimes deadly combination. If you suspect your child is drinking, you should intervene immediately. Even if you don't, talking to your children about alcohol at an early age is important . . . and it may save their lives.

You may wonder, with so many illegal drugs available to kids these days, what's the big deal with alcohol? Shouldn't that be the least of our worries? Not at all. Alcohol is as much a drug as cocaine and cannabis and for children, it's just as illegal, and can be dangerous as well.

Children who drink are more likely to:

• Become victims of violent crime.
• Have trouble in school.
• Become involved in alcohol-related car accidents.

As a parent – or concerned adult – the main thing when dealing with children and alcohol is to trust your instincts. When talking with your pre-teen, choose words that are understandable to them; use ideas you are comfortable with. The conversation should not seem forced, but rather almost as if it is a spur-of-the-moment idea you've had. Talk to your child the same way you would talk to him about anything else he might be interested in. Your child – whether you realise it or not – looks to you for support and for guidance. Your attitudes and opinions shape and mould him in making his own life decisions, including his decision about using alcohol.

'Why worry now? My child is only ten. He's certainly not drinking yet!'

True, he may not be drinking yet. However, between the ages of ten and fourteen he is likely to begin experimenting with alcohol. It's best to talk to him about it before that happens. Even if he isn't drinking by this time, some of his friends may be. Peer pressure can be hard to avoid. Now is the time to talk to him – before you think he's drinking. Help him to form responsible attitudes toward alcohol. The best thing you can do is to act now; the worst you can do is keep quiet. Think about it. If you don't say anything to him about alcohol, instead of forming his opinions from yours, he'll form them based on what he's heard on the street. Wouldn't it be better for you, as his loving parent, to guide him to thinking responsibly about drinking?

Adolescence can be a trying time for a child. Hormones run rampant during this time. Not only do changes appear, but they appear rapidly. Do you remember your own puberty? You may have been between eleven and thirteen when the process began. Of course, your child may experience puberty even earlier than that. Hormones may cause him to be moody and restless. Girls tend to mature faster, but boys will catch up after a few years. For girls, the changes that occur are the start of menstruation, the appearance of hair growth under their arms and in the pubic area. For boys, puberty causes the growth of body and pubic hair, a deepening voice, and frequent erections. Both sexes experience rapid physical growth.

These changes can be quite stressful to your child as he attempts to adjust to them. In just a few short years, your child will be a young man or woman who is capable of having their own children. Still, they will need your support.

During puberty and adolescence, your child will need your reassurance and acceptance. Most of all, he will need your advice and your availability. He should feel that he can come and talk to you when he needs to. While this is an age where he will often turn to his friends for advice, it will be a help for him to know that he can also approach you as well.

Simply psychological

In addition to all the physical changes in puberty, teens also have to deal with psychological differences in the way they think and feel. They are not as dependent on their families for their relationships but now put a heavy emphasis on their friends. Parents aren't as important as they once were: their peers seem to have more of an influence on them. This is perfectly normal for their age and should be nothing to worry about. However, if their friends use alcohol or other drugs, that is cause for concern. You should definitely monitor your child and his friends and their activities.

Adolescence is a time when your child will begin to spread his wings. He wants to become more independent and feels that he is more grown up than he has ever been. He may argue and disagree with you as he forms his own views and opinions. This will be a time when you find your child on the telephone for long periods with their friends. They will also spend a lot of time on the computer chatting with each other. In fact, you may find they spend as much time chatting on-line as they do actually hanging out with each other.

At this stage of life, teens want to fit in with their peers. This is evidenced in their clothing and appearance. Remember when you were younger? You didn't wear the clothes your parents thought were 'cool.' Your children won't either. If their friends like it, they'll wear it. Likewise, if their friends offer them a drink, they may take it just to fit in. They don't want to appear 'uncool.' This is why it is so important to talk to your child about alcohol when he is young, so when the situation arises that he is offered alcohol, he'll have a choice of responses.

Don't get offended if you feel your child is rejecting you at this time. Children usually think highly of their parents, even when they disagree or are angry with them. No matter how many arguments you have with your child, realise that he is not necessarily attacking you personally, but just because you are the parent, and he is trying to break away and become more independent. At this time, it is normal for your child to feel very much like an adult one moment, and very much like a child in the next. Sometimes he will make adult decisions, and other times his decisions will be quite childish. This is another good reason you should talk to him about alcohol. Give him the ammo he needs to 'just say no' when offered a drink.

Simply put, adolescence is the time when your child gains an interest in learning about the world around him and how he fits into it. This may involve trying new things, including alcohol, just to experiment. However, if you've had conversations concerning alcohol and your child knows where you stand on underage drinking, he can draw from that knowledge and make wiser decisions.

Usually a child experiments with drinking among friends who are drinking. The child who drinks alone is more at risk of developing a long-term problem with alcohol.

Teen problems

Becoming a teen – and experiencing all the changes, both physical and emotional – isn't easy. If the teen chooses to drink alcohol, it only compounds the problems they are already dealing with in adolescence.

The following are signs that your child may be going through emotional distress:

- Depression: Your child may cry alone and feel that he just wants to get away from everything and everyone; he may feel that he does not want to live; he loses interest in things that once interested him.
- Eating disorders: Your child may overeat or become anorexic.
- Anxiety: Your child may seem over-anxious, even to the point of panic attacks.
- Excessive sleep: Your child may spend more time than necessary sleeping – this could also be a sign of depression.
- Obsessed with physical appearance: Your child may be overly concerned with his or her physical appearance.

Adolescence is also a time when a child experiences rapid physical changes that can cause them problems sexually. The dramatic changes can make a shy child extremely uncomfortable. On the other hand, some teens will brag excessively about their sexual ability and experiences, whether real or imagined. When teens reach the age of consent, they may assume it's okay to experiment sexually, although they may not be emotionally mature enough to handle the consequences or to make wise choices concerning sex.

Alcohol often goes hand in hand with underage sex; it would be surprising if it didn't . . . When it does, often the sex that occurs is not always consensual. Even without drinking, early age sex too often leads to pregnancy and health problems, such as HIV, AIDS, and other sexually transmitted diseases.

Behavioural problems are also another issue that adolescents face. Teens complain about their parents and parents complain about their teens. What was once a happy family unit may now be thrown into turmoil as the teen strives to assert his independence and freedom. Parents may find themselves questioning their parenting abilities. A key point to remember is to know where your child is and who he is with at all times. That can deter a greater problem, including whether or not your child chooses to use alcohol or illegal drugs. Also, parents should be clear about the rules they set and the consequences for breaking

Age of Consent to sex

England	16
Scotland	16
Wales	16
N. Ireland	17

Sex is illegal if either partner is under these ages, even if both give their consent.

those rules. Teens tend to test the boundaries during adolescence. However, at the same time they want their parents to set those boundaries.

Behavioural problems at home may carry over into the school, as can emotional problems. Sometimes a child will begin refusing to go to school or threaten to leave. This can be due to:

• Becoming depressed about poor results.
• Bullying.
• Pressure from teachers or parents to excel.
• Unhealthy family life.
• Friends who have dropped out of school.

It's also possible that alcohol has become a problem to the point that they have lost interest in their schoolwork and activities. Be sure to take that into consideration if your child has formed a lackadaisical attitude toward school.

This is the time when a child may get in trouble with the law. If the parents do not feel that breaking the law is important, the child is more likely to find themselves in trouble. Usually, boys are more apt to offend than girls. Usually they learn from their first brush with law enforcement; however, if you find your child is getting into trouble on a regular basis, there may be an underlying problem with drugs or alcohol.

As stated before, appearance is very important to an adolescent. If a teen feels he is overweight, he may go on a strict diet whether he really needs to or not. This is also true if he is facing criticism at school or being made fun of because of his weight. If depression seeps in, it can lead to inactivity and compound the problem. Plus, the child may turn to alcohol in his depression. It's important to be supportive of your child during the adolescent years to ensure they are content with who they are.

All of the above problems can lead into the teen turning to alcohol or drugs to cope or escape. Quite possibly, the reason for using alcohol is simply experimentation. It's actually not that common that teens form a regular use of drugs or alcohol in adolescence. However, when that does happen, the problems are only compounded. There is a good chance that if your teen is abusing drugs, he is abusing alcohol as well. While the alcohol may not seem quite as bad as using illicit drugs, the effects can be just as deadly.

The big question
What happens if your teen asks if you ever used alcohol when you were young? If the honest answer is 'no,' good for you. However, if you experimented with alcohol, you'll need to decide how best to respond. Generally, it's best to be honest, but you'll need to gauge the maturity level of your teen and whether or not he will use that information as an excuse to drink himself. Above all, if you do admit you drank alcohol while under age, don't just laugh it off. That will give the impression it's not that important. Stress the importance of not drinking and show him the serious consequences that underage drinking may lead to.

The process of growing up and becoming an adult can be quite challenging. However, with parental support and guidance, you child can make the transition with fewer roadblocks than if you weren't a crucial part of his life.

Even if you find your child does have an alcohol problem, don't feel that you have failed. Take it from there and get help.

First of all, remain calm. Make sure of your facts. And, never . . .

• Put the blame on them or their friends – you'll lose their confidence.
• Get into arguments when they have been drinking.
• Give up – keep on loving and supporting them.

Help!
You find your child has been abusing alcohol and you aren't sure what to do next. First, you may want to have a confidential talk with your GP. He can give you information and advice on local agencies that can help with support and treatment. You may also want to contact these:

• Your child's teachers.
• Your child's school nurse.
• Youth workers
• Local police.
• Social workers.
• Drug and alcohol agencies.

You'll find that helping your child cope with the problems of adolescence is both admirable and satisfying.

When friends go bad
While parents do have an influence on their children, it is often their friends who have the greatest influence in terms of attitudes and values. If his friends drink, your child is more likely to drink. It is hard, during adolescence, for a child to say 'no' to his friends. However, open communication between him and his parents makes it easier.

Friendships during the teen years are completely different from the relationship a child has with his parents. At times, they involve more sharing and intimacy. Teens are more willing to talk about themselves and their feelings with their peers. They also are open to sharing their problems and giving advice to each other. And they are more apt to take a friend's advice than a parent's. Close friends will share the most intimate details of their lives with each other until they actually feel closer to the friend than to their family members. You will find that in an effort to define their own uniqueness, it seems they are imitating each other's styles in clothing, hairstyle, mannerisms, taste in music, and drug and alcohol use.

Teenage girls put a lot of emphasis on loyalty and support in their one-on-one friendships. As they mature, more intimacy and acceptance of differences is evident in friendships. Teenage boys never seem to reach the intimacy level of girls. Groups of friends are more important to them than the one-on-one intimate relationships. Either way, friends are very influential on your child, and his values may be shaped by the kinds of friendships he makes during this time. Therefore, it is important to keep tabs on what kinds of friends your child is hanging out with.

The brain game
When a child enters adolescence, we notice the drastic physical changes right away. What we don't notice is the changes in the child's neural system. During these years, the brain's progressive

formation is critical. If alcohol is introduced, and used on a regular basis, it may cause brain damage.

Think of the brain as a work in progress. By the time a child reaches adolescence, his brain isn't completely what it will be by the time he reaches adulthood. A teenager's brain is designed to learn life skills by acquiring information and adapting it to different situations. Heavy consumption of alcohol – particularly alcohol-dependence – can interrupt this process, thus making it difficult for the child to master certain skills even after he becomes an adult.

As you can see, teenage drinking can pose all sorts of problems. It is up to you, as a responsible adult, to curb your child's drinking as much as possible, and to give him good reasons why he should not drink.

Tips for parents

Make and enforce rules concerning alcohol. Make sure the rules are clear to all family members and that they are consistent. Make sure they are reasonable and that the consequences for breaking them are reasonable: i.e., losing privileges, suspension of allowance, etc.

- Make your home safe. While adolescents are eager to experiment, your drinks cupboard may be too much of a temptation. Keep your alcohol under lock and key to ensure your home is safe for your child and his friends.
- Make yourself available. Keep the communication lines open between you and your child. Let him know that he can come and talk to you at anytime. Not only that, but look for opportunities to talk to him, even about things you don't feel are important. This will keep the communication open for the times when you need to discuss heavier issues, such as alcoholism.
- Be sure to back up the other parent. Parents need to support each other in decisions made concerning their children. This is all-important during the teen years. Teenagers will know if one of you is more lenient concerning the rules than the other. Never ally yourself with your child against the other parent. As parents, you need to stand firm and be supportive of each other to gain your child's respect.
- Pick your battles with your teen. There are many things that teenagers will do that are simply irritating to their parents. Many of these are not worth arguing about. Focus on praising their good behaviour and decisions. When it comes to disagreements, make sure the subject matter warrants a heavy discussion.

'Like father, like son'

While it seems that friendships among other adolescents take priority over the parent's influence, your child will watch you and from time to time mimic you. If you drink heavily, he may become curious and want to try alcohol, too. If you do drink, make sure you drink responsibly and moderately and set a good example for your child.

Just whose kids are using alcohol anyway?

Alcohol consumption among teens has no preference. Whether your teen is upper class or lower class or somewhere in between, he is still at risk for using alcohol and drugs. He may experiment simply to see what it's like to feel intoxicated. Sometimes, it's due to peer pressure. Alcohol does not just affect someone else's kids; it can affect your kids, too.

The dangers

One of the particular dangers of alcohol experimentation is the combination of alcohol with drugs. Some of the drugs or other substances your teen may become involved with are:

Cigarettes

- While mixing cigarettes with alcohol is not necessarily any more dangerous than smoking and drinking separately, cigarettes cause their own set of diseases with cancer, heart disease, and high blood pressure at the top of the list. They are also highly addictive and many teens who do choose to smoke become addicted by adulthood.

Cannabis (marijuana)

- This is the most common illegal drug among teens. The herbal form is known as grass or weed; it usually looks like dried herbs, sometimes with seeds. The more concentrated form, known as resin or hash, looks like lumps of brown or black shoe polish. Users smoke it – frequently mixed with tobacco – or bake it into cakes. Effects include euphoria, lethargy and a hunger for junk food. Panic attacks and longer-term mental problems can also develop.

Ecstasy

- A highly addictive drug that comes in tablets of different colours and shapes. It makes the user feel lively and happy, or sometimes anxious and scared. It's easy to become overheated and dehydrated while taking ecstasy which can lead to death. Contrariwise, worrying about dehydration can cause excessive water intake which in extreme cases can also lead to death.

Glue/aerosols

- These substances are sometimes sniffed to get 'high.' They can give a false courage, causing people to do things they normally would not do. They can also cause hallucinations, sick or sleepy feelings, and can cause the heart to stop.

Amphetamines

- Also known as speed, uppers or Billy Whiz. This comes as a white or yellowish powder, or as tablets. Can be swallowed, injected, or sniffed. The stronger (and more addictive) methamphetamine (Crystal meth) can also be smoked. Users may feel energetic, that they have a 'buzz.' They may also be very talkative, or scared and experience hallucinations. As a stimulant, amphetamines can affect the heart adversely.

LSD

- Also known as acid. It comes on small pieces of paper. LSD is either eaten or held in the mouth to dissolve. The 'trip' LSD users experience may be either pleasant or scary. They hallucinate, seeing strange colours and shapes, and may hear noises. Even months after taking LSD, the user is susceptible to flashbacks.

Cocaine (also known as coke or snow) and crack cocaine (also known as rock).

- A white powder that is generally sniffed, this drug makes people feel lively and confident (though to non-users they may just seem self-centred and boring). Crack is actually the size of a baked bean as crystals and is smoked. The effects are more rapid and intense than regular cocaine. Both forms are highly addictive and can cause chest pains and difficulty in breathing.

Tranquilisers
• These come as capsules or tablets that are either eaten or injected. They are different colours and shapes. They are addictive and may make the user drowsy, relaxed, and sleepy.

Heroin
• Also known as smack. It is a brownish white powder that is smoked, sniffed, or injected. It is highly addictive and can be fatal, and makes people feel disconnected with the world around them.

Anabolic steroids
• These are tablets or liquids that are injected into a muscle or swallowed. Users take them to improve muscle mass, but they can cause serious health problems such as hormonal problems and depression. Boys taking anabolic steroids have been known to experience breast development; girls taking them have had excessive body hair growth.

As you can imagine, taking any of these in combination with alcohol could be a deadly mix. Your teen may choose alcohol – at first – and 'graduate' to harder drugs later on. Alcohol itself may give him a relaxed and confident feeling and may become addictive with continued use. In some users, it causes miserable feelings. Remember that alcohol does affect the liver, nervous system, and brain, particularly in adolescents whose systems are not yet mature. Also, if your teen is drunk – aside from the physical effects – he can get into all kinds of trouble, from fighting, to unsafe sex, to car accidents, to trouble with the law.

The good news
Adolescence has had a bad press. However, recent studies have shown that most teenagers actually like their parents and feel that they get on well with them. It is a time when the process of growing up can help people to make positive changes, and to put the problems of the past behind them.

It is not just a difficult stage, although it can feel very much like it at times. The anxiety experienced by parents is more than matched by the periods of uncertainty, turmoil and unhappiness experienced by the adolescent.

Difficult times come and go, but most adolescents don't develop serious problems. It's worth remembering this when things are difficult.

Parents may sometimes start to feel that they have failed. However, whatever may be said in the heat of the moment, they play a crucial part in their children's lives. Helping your children grow through adolescence can be profoundly satisfying.

It's the time many children yearn to experiment and try new things. Some of the reasons young teens drink alcohol are:

• Out of curiosity.
• Peer pressure.
• To feel grown up.
• Because it feels good.
• To fit in with their friends.

Unfortunately, it is impossible to know which teens will stop drinking and which ones will continue and eventually become alcohol-dependent. Adolescents have a natural tendency to feel indestructible; they think they are immune to becoming hooked on drugs or alcohol: it's always going to happen to someone else, but never to them. Experimenting with illegal substances has always been common among teens and pre-teens. And often they cannot see the consequences of their actions until it's too late. That is why it is so important that you talk to your teen or pre-teen.

While we can't know which teens will go on to abuse alcohol, there are several key factors which indicate a teen is more at risk for alcohol-dependency:

• Those who are depressed.
• Those who have low self-esteem.
• Those who are loners and feel like they don't fit in.
• Those who have a family member who abuses alcohol.

Contrary to what you may think, teenagers do care what their parents think, even if they don't show it. If you show that you disapprove of them using alcohol, your children may choose not to drink based on that premise. In fact, parents' disapproval is a key reason many children do choose not to drink. Never, ever think that you can't make a difference – you can!

Do you suspect your child of abusing alcohol?
Use the following checklist to see if you have cause for worry.

• He is tired a lot, has trouble sleeping, has a cough that doesn't clear up, and his eyes are glazed and red.
• His behaviour is irresponsible; he has low self-esteem coupled with poor judgement. He has sudden mood swings and seems depressed, lacking interest in activities he was formerly interested in.
• He has become a discipline problem at school and has a negative attitude, does not care when he gets bad exam results. He has many absences and skips classes.
• He has begun arguing with you and other family members, then withdraws from the family. He breaks rules you have set and acts as though he doesn't care.
• He exhibits a change in his appearance, including the way he dresses. He hangs out with people who are involved in drugs or alcohol. He has begun having problems with the police.

Now, the above criteria may not necessarily indicate alcohol use in your child. It could indicate another kind of drug abuse, or it may point to emotional problems. The main thing is . . . if you see your teen exhibiting any symptoms like those listed, it's time to talk and to find out what the real problem is.

The number one drug of choice for teens is . . . you guessed it: alcohol. Probably because it is the most accessible. Think about it. Many of their parents drink, at least socially, so swiping a bit of alcohol now and then is a piece of cake. The fact is, alcohol is a more frequently used – and more heavily used – drug among teenagers than all other drugs combined. While it's true that the majority of kids under the age of fourteen have not begun to drink – at least no more than a sip or two – they are definitely at risk for experimenting and that is when you really need to talk to them about alcohol if you haven't before.

A few statistics . . .

- One fifth of children aged 13 to 14 report they have drunk alcohol.
- Seventeen out of one hundred say they have been drunk during the past year.
- Seventy-one out of one hundred believe that alcohol is easy to get.

It is a mistake to feel relief if your adolescent is 'just' drinking. Remember, alcohol is a drug. Not only that, but it is a mood-altering drug. Is that really something you want your child to be involved with? Of course not. Let's face it, teens have not developed the judgement to handle alcohol wisely. They also do not yet have coping skills to deal with alcohol and how it may affect them. Therefore:

- Car crashes involving alcohol are a major cause of death in adolescents.
- A high percentage of drowning among teens is linked to alcohol.
- A high percentage of suicide among teens is due to alcohol.
- A high percentage of murder among teens is alcohol-related.
- Teens using alcohol generally have sex at an earlier age than their non-drinking counterparts.
- Teens using alcohol generally have more unprotected sex than teens who do not drink, making them more susceptible to STIs and pregnancy.
- Teens who drink alcohol are more likely to become victims or perpetrators of violent crimes than those who do not drink.
- Teens involved with alcohol have more disciplinary problems in school and poorer results.
- Teens who drink are more likely to develop a dependence on alcohol than are people who wait to drink until they become adults.

No doubt, for young people, drinking alcohol puts them at risk for all kinds of problems. This is why it is important for you to broach the subject of drinking while your child is still young.

Alcohol is a major cause of car crashes among adolescents

PART  # The teenager's world

Adolescence is the time in a person's life when changes come quickly and dramatically. It can be challenging for both the teen and his parents. However, knowing what to expect can make the transition from childhood to adulthood a bit smoother.

What's happening?

Between the ages of ten and fourteen, children often experience drastic changes in their height and weight. These changes can occur so drastically that the child feels a bit awkward, as if he hasn't had time to adjust before he grows even more. Sexual development begins as well, causing children to become self-conscious and even uncomfortable with their own bodies. Unlike when they were younger, they now have an awareness of their physical appearance, often questioning whether they measure up to their peers.

Am I . . .

- Tall enough?
- Skinny enough?
- Strong enough?
- Pretty enough?

Sometimes teens don't feel that they fit in during this time. Their lack of self-confidence might contribute to these feelings as well as the many changes that are occurring. Sometimes, trying to please their friends or fit in, they will experiment with alcohol. Be sure to convey to your child that you are proud of them and that you love them during this time. Your words and actions can go a long way to increasing your child's self-esteem.

What was I thinking?

Even young teens often adopt the attitude that bad things only happen to other people. Still, they have matured to the point where they are beginning to understand that drinking alcohol does have consequences. They often live in the here and now and don't worry too much about what may happen later because of what they do 'right now.' This is a good time to emphasise the risks of drinking alcohol and the consequences that can occur if they do. Even if you have talked to your children when they were younger, it's a good idea to reiterate what you told them and to see how they now feel about alcohol consumption.

Why do I feel this way?

As mentioned earlier, fitting in with friends is all-important to an adolescent. During this time a parent may feel if he/she is being abandoned as the teen prefers to spend more time with friends than at home. This is perfectly normal. While the teen needs to know the parent's values and views on drinking and other issues, he may begin questioning those values and views and adopting the views of his friends instead. Conflict within the home is not uncommon during this time of early adolescence. Still, the parent should provide support as well as set appropriate limits, and, at the same time, respect the child's struggle for independence.

PART **The parent's role**

A good deterrent to your child using any type of drugs – including alcohol – is to form and maintain a strong parent-child relationship. Within such a relationship, the child will trust the parent and the parent's decisions and judgements. It has been proven that teens who have strong relationships with their parents are more likely to delay drinking or even abstain altogether. Even if the child does begin to drink, the closer the relationship to a parent, the more likely alcohol will not develop into a major problem for him.

Now, it is also true that adolescence brings conflict into the home as the child wants to spread his wings and become an independent person. If, during this time, the child's relationship with his parent has been distant or virtually non-existent, he may turn to drinking alcohol to gain the approval of friends or because of low self-esteem.

Children who have a close bond with their parent(s) tend to feel better about themselves. Still, they need your approval, support, and encouragement. In order to build a strong bond with your child, you first need to have a good rapport with him. Make sure the communication lines are open. Be ready and willing to talk when your child wants to talk. Encourage him to talk when he appears to be brooding. When talking with your child, guide him into responsible decision making when the subject of alcohol comes up.

If you are unsure on how to begin open communication with your teen, here are a few suggestions:

• Encourage your child to talk with you. Conversing about whatever interests your child and listening – really listening – will pave the way for your child to open up about topics that interest him and will make it easier for you to brooch the subject of alcohol.
• Ask questions, but not the simple 'yes' or 'no' kind. Give your child an opportunity to tell you how he is feeling and what he is thinking.
• Watch your reactions. It is important that you control the way you react to what your child is saying. You may not agree with his views, you may feel you need to defend your own or try to persuade him to your side. However, you should constructively talk with him, not putting him down, but still be open and honest with him. If you show you respect his point of view, he will be more willing to listen to yours.
• Emphasise his importance to you. Make sure you spend enough one-on-one time with him so he will realise how important he is to you. Show him, by listening, that you care about what he has to say. Spend time with him even when you aren't talking about 'important' subjects, such as alcohol-dependency. Share an activity, even if it's simply a walk around the block. Be together.

All time spent together is 'quality time'; it doesn't have to be serious

- Set guidelines. While you want to respect his opinions, you also need to let him know what you expect of him. Set rules and establish consequences if they are broken. Clarify what he should expect if he breaks the rules.
- Appreciate your child. Refrain from criticism or cruel teasing. Let your child know you care about him, his accomplishments, and his efforts.

Adhering to the above criteria will go a long way to establishing a good rapport and a good relationship with your child. This is key is forming a solid relationship foundation that you can build on and will make it easier to discuss such difficult subjects as alcohol usage.

Reasons not to drink? Who needs 'em?

Your child does! If, during the conversation with your teen about alcohol, you find he is asking why he shouldn't drink, these may be good to use:

- Drinking at his age is illegal.
- Drinking can be dangerous.
- Drinking can interfere with his school work.
- Drinking can rob him of self-respect.
- Drinking when under age is not an activity you approve of.

The talk

Many parents find the subject of alcohol to be a difficult matter to discuss. However, it's important to find ways to talk about it. Even when you do, your teen may try to dodge the discussion making it hard to know how to proceed. Be sure – before you even begin – that you have thought it through carefully. Think about all the ways your child may try to worm his way out of the conversation, and come up with solutions beforehand. Next, think about the ways your child may react to what you have to say. Consider positive reactions and negative ones. Think of how you will respond.

Think of the questions he may ask. What if he asks, 'Did you drink when you were a kid?' How would you handle this question? Let's face it . . . many of us did drink when we were teens, sneaking a little wine from our parents' cupboards or attending parties where alcohol was plentiful. If this is true of you, should you be completely honest, then sum it up by a 'do as I say, not as I do' statement? Obviously, this is up to you. You know your teen better than anyone does and how he might react. You may not want to share the details of your teen life with your child. On the other hand, you may want to share it and any negative experiences that occurred. Then you can sum up the conversation by telling him you want to save him the same embarrassing or painful moments.

One of the most important roles parents can play is to talk to their children about the hazards associated with alcohol. When discussing alcohol and the consequences of underage drinking, don't overlook the teenage deaths from alcohol-related car crashes. Talk to your child about the dangers of driving while impaired and also about riding with other teens who are driving drunk. Make sure they have enough money for a taxi or enough to call you should they not have a safe ride home.

There are many accidents and injuries which result from alcohol use. Many of these affect teens. Even low doses of alcohol impair the skills of those who consume it to the point that operating a vehicle is more difficult than if the driver were completely sober. Add to that the fact that teens are less experienced and haven't acquired the skills of a seasoned driver, and you have a deadly combination. Of course, there are other factors that can impair a teen's driving abilities as well, such as emotional states, fatigue, talking on cell phones, distractions by others in the vehicle, and illness. Adding alcohol consumption into the mix would not be wise under any of these circumstances.

When talking with your teen, don't feel like you have to cover everything at once. In fact, it may be better not to. You'll probably have a greater impact on your child if you have several talks about drinking rather than one big major conversation. Again, make sure the setting is comfortable to both you and your child. When you first broach the subject of alcohol consumption, think of it as the first part of a continuing discussion.

Remember those lectures your teachers would give that were so absolutely boring you could hardly stay awake? Remember how you hardly knew what they had said even a short while after you'd heard it? You had simply zoned out. Be sure when talking to your child, he does not tune out in the middle of your conversation. If he does, you may be guilty of giving a lecture rather than having a two-way conversation. If you feel you may go into 'lecture' mode with your child, take a look at the following suggestions for keeping it conversational.

• Ask your child what his opinion is about teen drinking.
• Ask what he knows about alcohol.
• Ask him why he thinks teens drink in the first place.

Finding out where he stands will help you to determine how you should lead the conversation. However, don't bombard him with questions one after the other. Keep the tone conversational. You ask; he shares; you share. Once you get to the point – and this may be after you've had several discussions about alcohol – where you feel you should give him some cold hard facts, try to dispel any myths he may have heard concerning alcohol.

Some of the fallacies he may have heard and believed to be true are:

- Beer and wine are safer than spirits.
- Taking a cold shower helps you sober up faster.
- Drinking black coffee helps you sober up faster.
- Walking it off will help get the alcohol out of your system.
- I'm too young to get addicted to alcohol.

If your child believes any of the above statements, make sure you let him know they are not true.

Alcohol is a strong drug. It affects the body and mind and slows down response time. It not only impairs vision, but also the way your mind thinks. It hampers your coordination. Spirits are not necessarily more dangerous than beer or wine. If your teen thinks that, he may feel it's okay to drink more beer and wine because it's 'safer.' However, a half pint of beer, a 125 ml glass of wine, and a standard measure of spirits will impair your teen to the same degree and contain much the same amount of alcohol. Neither taking a cold shower, drinking coffee, or walking it off will cause the alcohol to leave the body significantly faster. A single drink will take two to three hours to leave your system no matter how much you walk, drink coffee, or freeze in the shower. Finally, contrary to what some teens may think, teenagers are susceptible to alcohol-dependency as much as an adult.

Sometimes teens think drinking alcohol is cool, that it will make them more popular or more attractive. If they are lonely or depressed, they may feel that alcohol will make them happy. After all, they don't feel quite as lonely or depressed when they drink. However, just as with adults, their problems are still there when they sober up. If a teen expects positive results from drinking alcohol, he will be more likely to drink it. That's why it's so important for you, as a parent, to talk with your children and let them know the truths surrounding alcohol consumption.

Often teens get the impression drinking is cool from watching television and movies. You can help by watching with them and discussing how alcohol is portrayed on-screen. Not only that, but watch the advertisements for alcohol and beer. You'll see that many times young people are depicted as having a good time while drinking. No wonder your teen believes alcohol will enhance his life! These advertisements are finely honed by professional public relations people to do just that – entice people to want to buy their product. That's what they get paid for! Keeping an on-going discussion with your child will help him to see that drinking alcohol is not always what it is shown as.

If you have a family history of alcohol-dependency, you'll need to discuss this with your child. Chances are, your child may already be aware of what is going on if the problem is current. Explain to him that he may be more at risk because of their relative's dependency on alcohol. He needs to know this.

But everybody's doing it!

Ah, the joys of peer pressure. Talking to your teen about avoiding alcohol is not enough. You can talk until you are blue in the face and fill your child's head with good factual information, but if you don't show him the way to avoid alcohol, you've done him a disservice.

Let's go back in time. Remember what life was like as a teen. Think of the ways you were pressured to drink alcohol. No matter what your response, you can draw on your experience to find ways to help your teen say 'no' to alcohol. It's important that your teen knows how to respond when he's attending a party where beer is being served. Or maybe he is visiting a friend's house and a bottle of wine is being passed around. Will he know how to handle the pressure to drink? Will he know how to respond? What happens when your teen is offered a ride home from someone who has been drinking? Will he know what to do? He will if you have talked to him about it beforehand.

Talk to your teen about these situations. Get his feedback and try to come up with good responses together. Make sure the conversation is not one-sided. Make sure you allow him to give you his ideas. He knows the teen culture and the 'language' of teenagers, and you may be surprised at how well he comes up with appropriate responses.

It's inevitable. During his teen years, your child *will* be offered alcohol. Many times it's easier to resist the pressure by knowing the appropriate response. The more prepared he is, the better the chance that he will handle the situation correctly.

Above all, emphasise the point that you will back him up and support him. You can do this by offering to pick him up – anytime, at any hour – if he finds himself at a home where drinking occurs. Also, emphasise if you do pick him up, you won't scold or punish him.

Party on!

A good way to show your child and his friends a good time without alcohol is to host a party for them. Get together with your child and help him make up a guest list. Let him know that only those on the list will be admitted to the party – no gatecrashers! Discuss the rules, up front, so your child will know just what is expected of him and his friends. You may want to suggest that your child pick a friend to help him plan the party. Help him think of good activities that will keep the guests occupied. Let him know that if anyone tries to bring in alcoholic beverages, he'll be asked to leave. Make sure you have plenty of snacks and non-alcoholic drinks. A teen's appetite can be voracious.

On the night of the party, make sure you are visible, but curb your enthusiasm for joining the party. This is a *teen* party. Stay in the background and make sure your child knows you are available should he need you. Your supportive involvement will help your teen avoid underage drinking problems and ensure he and his friends have a good time as well.

PART

Taking action and making a difference

Talking with your teen and being an active part in his life goes a long way to keeping him from making irresponsible decisions concerning alcohol consumption. Teens like to think of themselves as 'grown up,' however, they are often not mature enough to make responsible decisions, given the pressures of their peers and their own curiosity. They still need adult supervision whether they think they do or not. The following list gives suggestions on how you can provide good supervision and guidance for your teen:

Alcohol in your home
If you keep alcohol in your own home, you should keep a good track of your supply, even if you're 'sure' your teen would never drink it. Make sure your teen knows he should not have friends over when an adult is not home. Still, it is good to have your teen entertain in your home where you can monitor him and his friends. Therefore you should encourage him to invite his friends over so you will become familiar with them and their activities.

Parental connection
Once your teen begins 'hanging out' at his friends' homes, you'll want to get acquainted with his friends' parents. Find out how closely they supervise teen gatherings in their homes. Find out if they allow parties that are not chaperoned. Make sure they do not allow alcohol at their parties before allowing your teen to attend. You may find that other parents share your concern about alcohol as well.

Do you know where your teen is?
It is important to keep a check on your teen's activities and plans. Teens are less likely to get into trouble if they know their parent could pop up at any given time. Also, set a curfew. Make sure he is certain of what time he needs to be home and to call you if he won't make it.

Rules
Now is the time to establish rules about not drinking. Let your teen know that underage drinking is not only wrong, but in some circumstances illegal, and will not be condoned. Have open communication and rules about drinking so that your young adults understand what alcohol is, how to drink moderately and that it is best consumed with a meal in sensible amounts, as part of a social interaction.

Some other family rules to consider may be:

- If alcohol is being served at a teenage party, the teen will call or come home.
- Teens will not ride with a driver who has been drinking.
- Teens will not accept alcohol from friends or siblings.

Rules are not enough. Once set, the consequences of breaking the rules should be discussed. This will give your teen an incentive not to break the rules. Also, enforcement of the punishments you set is key. If a teen finds out he can break the rules and get away with it, he is more likely to continue to break the rules and will have no respect for your authority.

Once you have established consequences, you must enforce them. This is key to having your rules work for you and your teen. If a child knows that certain privileges will be lost, it may deter him from taking action that would lose those privileges. And, most importantly, set a good example before him. If you drink, do it responsibly. Never drive when you have been drinking, even if you are not legally drunk. You are your child's best role model. If you drink, know that most children who drink were raised by parents who drink. However, there are steps you can take that may encourage your child to wait until adulthood to begin drinking:

- Never drink to the point where you become intoxicated. Keep your alcohol consumption to moderate levels. Remember, control your drinking, don't let it control you.
- Don't use alcohol as a way to cope with difficult situations. In other words, don't say, 'Man, I've had a tough day. I need a drink.' Use other ways to cope with stress, such as rational discussions with your spouse, exercise, reading quietly, or relaxing in a warm bath.
- Don't share funny stories about alcohol with your kids. The idea you want to convey about drinking alcohol is the seriousness of its negative affects, not the humour of daddy falling down drunk.
- Not only should you not drive when you've been drinking, you should make it a point not to ride with a driver who's been drinking.
- When you entertain in your home for other adults, be sure to offer plenty of non-alcoholic beverages in addiction to alcohol. Act responsibly: if someone drinks too much at your function, make sure he gets home safely.
- Never support underage drinking. Your attitude toward teenage drinking will go a long way to help your teen to make the choice to say 'no' to alcohol. Joking about teenage drinking will weaken your arguments against it. Don't be a parent who contributes to the problem by serving drinks to your teen and his friends. Not only can this be illegal, but teens who are served alcohol by adults tend to drink more heavily and thus are at greater risk of becoming involved in fatal car crashes.
- Encourage your child to build healthy friendships. Monitor his friends – know who they are, who their parents are, and if they subscribe to the same standards that you do. It's more likely your child will drink if his friends do. Therefore, it makes good sense to help your child develop relationships with teens who do not drink. Also, make your home available for gatherings of your child's friends. If your child already has undesirable friends, it can be tough to handle. If you forbid your child to hang out with that friend, it may make him more eager to hang

around him. The best course of action would be to talk to your child, in a conversational manner, about the reservations you have about their friend. Don't be accusing, just show that you really care about the influence this child has on yours. You can also find ways to limit your child's contact with certain friends by forming rules about how after school time should be spent or how late they can stay out.

- Keep your teen busy. Boredom can be an excuse for drinking. If he has plenty of challenging activities, he will have less time to be bored. Your community or school may offer sports programmes or other activities that your teen is interested in. Be sure to talk to him and find out what his interests are rather than pushing him into an activity that does not interest him at all.

Is your child at risk?

It's true that some children are more likely than others to begin drinking and to abuse alcohol and suffer negative consequences. These consequences may include problems with health, family, school, and law enforcement. Use the following checklist to see if your child is at a high risk for alcohol-related problems:

- One or both parents are alcohol-dependent.
- The child's friends drink alcohol.
- Parental discipline is harsh or hostile.
- There are behavioural problems.
- They are failing in school.
- Began drinking alcohol before 15 years old.
- They exhibit aggressive or antisocial behaviour.

If you find your child has one or more of these risk factors, it does not necessarily mean that he will go on to develop an alcohol problem. It does mean that you may need to begin talking to him and forming a plan to protect him from influences that may lead to heavy drinking. Re-read *The parent's role* section and begin talking to your teen and listening to his ideas on teen drinking. If your child exhibits most of the above risk factors, you may need to seek professional help. Your child's GP or school could help you determine what course of action to take depending on the severity of the problem.

If you suspect your child already has a drinking problem, it's not too late to step in and help. Your healthcare professional can help you figure the best course of action even before you begin talking with your teen. However, if you've already established a good rapport with your child, it will help him in accepting any other course of action you take.

So, you think your child has a drinking problem . . .

There are signs that may indicate your child has a problem with alcohol or other drugs. However, it can be difficult to determine as many 'signs' simply reflect the normal teenager's development. The following are signs to look for and the more your teen

exhibits – and the more severe they are – the more likely that he may have a problem with alcohol/drugs.

- Quick temper or mood swings; irritable.
- Unkempt appearance.
- Low energy; lethargic.
- Secretive about new friends.
- Defensive.
- Poor exam results.
- Skipping school.
- Breaking family rules.
- Bloodshot eyes; slurred speech.
- Problems with memory and concentration.
- Presence of alcohol in your child's room.

Time to take action

The key to helping your child make the right choices concerning alcohol boils down to establishing a good, trusting relationship with him. Before the situation gets out of hand, it's a good idea to talk with him, listen to him, spend time with him, and above all, let him know the avenues of communication are always open. Find ways to make it easy for your child to talk with you. Give him plenty of opportunities in the activities you plan, the time you spend together. Above all, set a good example for him to follow while keeping tabs on his activities and friends.

Parents can best help their child through providing early education about drugs and alcohol, open communication, positive role modelling and early recognition and treatment of emerging problems.

For further information

Positive Parenting provides parenting workshops, literature, resources and training programmes for parents and professionals.

Website: www.parenting.org.uk

ChildLine provides a free and confidential service for children.

Website: www.childline.org.uk

Parentline offers helpful advice to parents of children and teens.

Website: www.parentlineplus.org.uk

Raising Kids provides a website for parents.

Website: www.raisingkids.co.uk

The Samaritans offers emotional support for anyone in a crisis.

Tel: 08475 909090

E-mail: jo@samaritans.org

Website: **www.samaritans.org**

Al-Anon – for the families of alcohol abusers.

Website: www.al-anonuk.org.uk

Talk to Frank – for information on all recreational drugs, legal or not.

Website: **www.talktofrank.com**

Odds and ends

Photo: © iStockphoto.com, Ina Peters

Adult children of alcoholics

When a child grows up in a dysfunctional home, he will be affected. Alcohol-dependency by one parent or both will cause a type of dysfunction within the family unit. As the child matures into an adult, he may or may not know how to function normally in society, in a family unit, or in the workplace. Some remain in an emotional or psychological childhood of sorts, never having really grown up and matured. They had no good 'normal' example to draw on, because they were brought up by people who had never really grown up themselves. Thinking, feeling, and reacting to different situations are now, as an adult, a real challenge.

Some adult children of alcoholics will:

- Feel they are different from others around them.
- Not know how to have fun.
- Find themselves in unhealthy or abusive relationships.
- Lie for no apparent reason.
- Overreact emotionally when under stress.
- Become either irresponsible or excessively responsible.
- Exhibit misplaced loyalty.
- Judge themselves harshly.

This cycle can continue as they begin to develop relationships and have families of their own. However, it does not have to be that way. With a good support system and possibly professional help, adult children of alcoholics can lead a normal, happy life.

Photo: © iStockphoto.com, Marcel Pelletier

The obsessive mind

Alcohol-dependence can make your mind become obsessive about taking a drink. This is particularly true if you have given up drinking completely. When you aren't drinking, it is constantly on your mind. The key to combating this effectively is to fill up your mind – and your time – with other things. However, sometimes, as hard as you try, the drink that calls to you will just not go away.

It's rather like a song that gets stuck in your head. You try to get it out, but it keeps coming back. You turn on the radio, you play a CD, you hum another tune. Still, that same song keeps on playing. Your mind is obsessed with the song.

In the same way, the drink calling to you keeps coming back over and over again. You feel powerless to cast it out of your head. More so, you feel a physical drawing to it. Now, the obsession has got to the point that you feel the only way to remedy the situation is to take a drink. At first, one or two drinks will curb the obsession. However, soon, it takes a few more . . . then more . . . soon you are drinking till you pass out just to keep the obsession under control.

The need for a drink is always on your mind

Illustration: © iStockphoto.com, Ian Witham

As you go through recovery, some things that may help you keep your mind from becoming obsessed with drinking are to:

- Take up a hobby.
- Build something.
- Start a collection.
- Play a sport.
- Sign up for an exercise class.
- Go fishing.
- Take online classes.
- Write your memoirs.
- Plant a garden.
- Volunteer at a local school.
- Get involved in a charity.
- Get involved in your church.

Staying busy and doing worthwhile things will keep your mind occupied and give you an opportunity to improve yourself and make a contribution to society. And don't forget to spend more time with your family. It may be hard to make up for all the hours you spent at the pub or in a drunken state, but you can try by making a brand new start.

Do something practical to keep your mind off drinking

PART 12

Trauma and alcohol

According to the dictionary, trauma is defined as a serious injury or shock to the body, as from violence or an accident. It is a major cause of injury and death worldwide. Many cases of trauma are alcohol-related.

According to Lowenfels and Miller (1984), alcohol intoxication is associated with 40 to 50 percent of traffic fatalities; 25 to 35 percent of non-fatal motor vehicle injuries; up to 64 percent of fires and burns; 48 percent of hypothermia and frostbite cases; and about 20 percent of suicides in the United States.

People can still have accidents even when they are not 'legally' drunk. They may fall and injure themselves, or they may get behind the wheel and injure themselves and others. Sometimes alcohol's 'loosening up' effect gives the drinker a false sense of courage and they take actions they normally would not take – for instance, suicides and murders. Many accidents could be prevented and many lives could be saved if only the drinker could control his drinking or eliminate it completely.

The task

It is hard to determine the precise role alcohol has in trauma events due to the differences in various studies. However, it has been determined that approximately a third of injury cases presenting at casualty departments are alcohol-related. About a quarter of all people hospitalised with an injury have problems with controlling their alcohol consumption. This is something the consumer of alcohol should be aware of. Once drinking gets out of hand, there is greater risk for personal injury and injury to others.

Not only are drinkers more likely to be involved in accidents than non-drinkers, they are also likely to suffer more serious injuries. There is a popular belief that people who are intoxicated are more likely to survive serious accidents because of their 'relaxed' state; however, there are no facts to support this.

The alcohol factor and diagnosis

Let's say you have gone to casualty because of an accident. Of course you want the best medical care they could give. However, under the influence of alcohol, you may be misdiagnosed. A doctor's diagnosis, especially initially, depends on the symptoms exhibited by the patient. The symptoms of drunkenness often mimic symptoms of other problems. For example, slurred speech or memory lapses may appear as an indication of head injuries or stroke. On the other hand, if the doctor knows the patient is intoxicated, he may think all the symptoms presented relate to alcohol and may miss possible life-threatening conditions. It can also be dangerous to administer anaesthesia to drunken patients, which may cause much-needed surgery to be delayed until blood alcohol levels have fallen.

Alcohol may also affect the potency of certain drugs and will need to be considered in any decision the doctor makes regarding medications or anaesthesia. If a person is alcohol-dependent, he may have an imbalance in electrolytes (substances required by our cells to regulate the electric charge and flow of water molecules across cell membranes) and fluids. He may also have problems with his blood clotting properly and his liver function. If he experiences any withdrawal symptoms from his alcohol dependence, they only compound any medical problems he has.

In order to properly diagnose and treat a person who has experienced some type of physical trauma, a casualty doctor should order a blood alcohol test. This will give him the information he needs as to whether the patient has high levels of alcohol in his blood or not. Without the tests, misdiagnosis could result, as mentioned above.

When a patient has been stabilised and has been determined to be an alcohol abuser, the doctor should ideally refer him for treatment. Treatment needs vary depending on how severely addicted the abuser is. Sometimes treatment may include minimal intervention, or it may take the form of more intensive treatment. Referring a patient for treatment is the best way the doctor can serve his patient and society. The sooner a person gets help and learns to control his drinking, the sooner the rewards of living a fuller, more satisfying life.

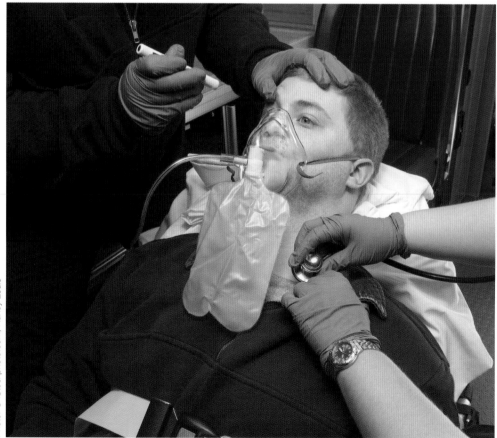

A menacing mixture

If you're taking medication, be it prescription or over-the-counter drugs, you may endanger your health by drinking alcohol. Some medications interact with alcohol in a way that can lead to an increased risk of physical illness, injury, or even death. Most people take prescription drugs at one time or another in their lifetime. If they are prone to taking a drink or drinking heavily, they may ignore or fail to notice the warnings on the drug packaging. This can be hazardous to the health.

The elderly are especially at risk. Statistically, elderly persons are more likely to suffer medication side-effects than younger people, and the effects become more pronounced with age.

A deadly duo

Drugs are prescribed in order to treat symptoms or effect a cure for disease. In order to have the desired effect, a drug usually travels through the bloodstream to an organ or tissue where it is then metabolised (processed) by enzymes. The medication is then eliminated from the body. Does this sound familiar? Alcohol behaves in much the same way. It is absorbed by the bloodstream and acts upon organs, such as the brain, causing drunkenness. Then it is eliminated from the body, mostly by the liver.

If you drink alcohol in conjunction with taking medication, it may inhibit the drug's metabolism. Think of it as a competition with your medication and your alcohol on opposite teams. The more the alcohol works against the drug, the more likely you are to experience severe side-effects. Even worse is when long-term heavy drinking is thrown into the mix. Think of that as Team Alcohol starting the game even before Team Medicine takes the field. If long-term drinking has activated an organ's enzymes, even when drinking ceases, the effects will remain, sometimes for several weeks. Even worse than just diminishing a drug's effects, alcohol may transform certain drugs into toxic substances that can actually damage your liver or other organs.

Alcohol's effects on medications

Anaesthetics
• These drugs are used before surgery to cause a patient to be unconscious. Heavy drinking may make it necessary for the dosage of the anaesthetic to be increased, risking liver damage.

Antibiotics
• These drugs are effective in treating infections. With heavy drinking thrown into the mix, the patient may experience nausea, vomiting, headache, and even convulsions. The effectiveness of the medications may also be reduced. Some antibiotics such as Metronidazole can make you very ill if you consume alcohol.

Anticoagulants
• These drugs are used to slow the blood's ability to clot. This can reduce the risk of stroke. Heavy drinking affects anticoagulants to the point that a patient is at risk from life-threatening haemorrhages.

Antidepressants

- Alcohol-dependency and depression often go hand in hand. Alcohol can increase the sedative effect of some antidepressants. This would impair the mental skills required for (e.g.) driving. Some beers and wine can cause high blood pressure when combined with certain antidepressants.

Antihistamines

- These drugs are used to treat allergy symptoms. They may also be used to treat insomnia as well. Alcohol may intensify the sedation effect. In older adults, antihistamines may cause dizziness and act as a sedative; this effect is combined when taken while drinking alcohol.

Antipsychotic medications

- These drugs are used to lessen symptoms such as delusions and hallucinations. Heavy alcohol use may result in impaired coordination and potentially fatal breathing difficulties, as well as liver damage.

Anti-seizure medications

- These drugs are often prescribed for epileptics. Heavy alcohol consumption may reduce their effectiveness, thereby reducing the patient's protection against seizures.

Cardiovascular medications

- These drugs treat problems with the heart and circulatory system. Heavy alcohol consumption in conjunction with these medications may cause dizziness or fainting upon standing up. Alcohol may reduce the effectiveness of medications used to treat high blood pressure.

Diabetic medications

- Oral hypoglycaemic drugs are prescribed to some patients with diabetes for lowering blood sugar levels. Combined with these drugs, alcohol may cause nausea and headache.

Narcotic pain relievers

- These drugs (opiates) treat moderate to severe pain. The combination of opiates and alcohol enhances the sedative effect of both substances, increasing the risk of death from overdose.

Non-narcotic pain relievers

- Who hasn't taken aspirin and other non-prescription pain relievers? These are very often used by the elderly. Some cause stomach bleeding and prevent blood from clotting. Using alcohol in conjunction with these drugs can compound these effects. Gastric bleeding may occur, as can liver damage.

Enough said? People who drink alcohol need to be aware of the problems raised by combining it with prescription and over-the-counter drugs. Even small amounts of alcohol should not be ingested when taking certain medications. Always consult your GP or pharmacist before combining alcohol with your medications. Older people should be especially careful, as medical problems tend to multiply with age.

Alcohol poisoning

What is it?

Alcohol poisoning occurs when alcohol affects the part of the brain which controls involuntary actions such as breathing and the gag reflex (which prevents choking). Drinking more alcohol than you can handle may cause the alcohol to eventually stop these functions, causing death. Often someone who drinks excessive alcohol will vomit. This is because alcohol irritates the stomach. Then there is the danger that he may choke on his vomit, which would cause death by asphyxiation if the person has passed out.

A person's BAC can continue to rise even after he has become unconscious. Although he is out, his bloodstream is still circulating alcohol throughout his body. Many people assume the unconscious person will be fine – he just needs to sleep it off. This isn't true. When someone passes out due to excessive alcohol consumption, alcohol poisoning has occurred and help should be called.

How do I know if it's alcohol poisoning?

These are the signs:

- Slow breathing (fewer than eight breaths per minute).
- Mental confusion, stupor, coma, or person cannot be roused.
- Irregular breathing (10 seconds or more between breaths).
- Seizures.
- Vomiting.
- Hypothermia (low body temperature), bluish skin colour, paleness.

What should I do?

- Know the danger signals.
- Do not wait for all symptoms to be present.
- Be aware that a person who has passed out may die.
- If there is any suspicion of an alcohol overdose, call for help. Don't try to guess the level of drunkenness.

What if alcohol poisoning is not treated?

There is no best case scenario. If left untreated, a victim of alcohol poisoning can experience the following:

- Choking on his own vomit.
- Breathing will slow, become irregular, or stop.
- Heart beats irregularly or stops.
- Hypothermia (low body temperature) occurs.
- Hypoglycaemia (too little blood sugar) leads to seizures.
- Untreated severe dehydration from vomiting can cause seizures, permanent brain damage, or death.
- Even if the victim lives, an alcohol overdose may lead to brain damage that is irreversible.

Sometimes a person will choose to binge drink, particularly if they are associating with others who drink heavily. If not careful, he can ingest a fatal amount of alcohol, become unconscious, and die. Some people may laugh at the drunk who falls down unconscious. While it may be comical, what isn't funny is when someone chokes on his or her own vomit and dies.

Never hesitate to seek medical attention for someone who has had too much to drink. Don't worry that he may become angry or embarrassed. It's more important that you cared enough to help. Unfortunately, many young people regret not seeking medical help for a friend when they should have. Often feelings of guilt ensue for alcohol-related tragedies that could have easily been prevented.

If you notice someone has passed out, the best thing you can do is call for help. Doing so may save a life.

Photo: © iStockphoto.com, Jaimie Duplass

Artificial respiration

Check the area for danger, if safe kneel to one side of the casualty. Lean over the casualty and into each ear ask in a loud voice if they can hear you and to open their eyes for you. You can also gently shake the casualty's shoulders while doing so. If there is no response shout for help.

Open the airway by gently placing one hand on the casualty's forehead and two fingers under the chin and gently tilt the head backwards.

Check for normal breathing by placing your ear close to the casualty's mouth and looking at the chest for a rising and falling motion. Do this for no more than 10 seconds. If there is no response send or call for help. Ensure the rescue service knows that the casualty is unconscious and not breathing normally.

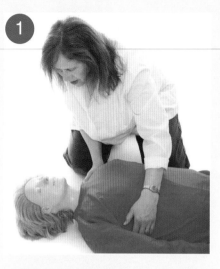

Give 30 chest compressions using two hands in the centre of the chest, at a rate of 100 per minute to a depth of 4 to 5 cms. If you think of the tune 'Nelly the Elephant' this will give you an idea of the pace the compressions need to be.

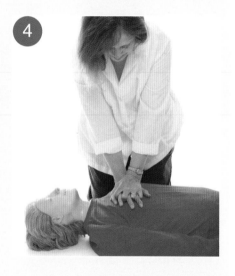

Attempt 2 rescue breaths. Seal your lips over the casualty's mouth and holding their nose deliver the breath over 1 second and remove your mouth then repeat once more. Continue artificial respiration with the correct ratio of 30 chest compressions to 2 rescue breaths. Continue until the rescue services tell you to stop or the patient begins to breath normally, in which case place them into the recovery position and monitor their responses until help arrives.

The recovery position

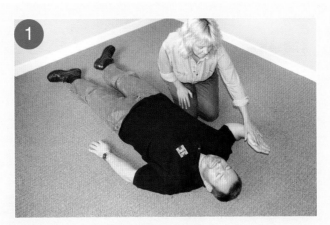

1. Make sure that the legs are straight and place the nearest arm at right-angles to the body

2. Hold the casualty's hand against the cheek, palm outwards, and raise the furthest leg, keeping the foot on the floor

3. Keeping the hand against the cheek, pull the raised leg and roll the casualty

4. Adjust the upper leg so that both hip and knee are at right-angles, and check that the hand below the cheek helps keep the airway open

The road to recovery

Ways to cut down on alcohol

Once you've made the decision to cut down on your alcohol consumption, the obvious question is . . . how?

Cutting down on alcohol can improve your life and your health. These suggestions may help you to achieve your goal.

Think of your reasons for curbing your alcohol consumption and write them down.

- What makes you want to drink less?
- Are you seeking to improve your health?
- Do you want to sleep better or be more alert when you're awake?
- Do you want to excel in your profession?
- Do you want to improve your relationships with your family members and friends?

> Drinking does not control me – I control my drinking!

Think of a realistic goal and focus on that. Maybe you've chosen not to drink at all. In that case, your goal might be to cut down day by day or week by week until you are no longer drinking. On the other hand, you may realise you are drinking too heavily and simply want to become a moderate drinker. Remember, if you are a woman, you should have no more than two units per day; and men should have no more than three. (These limits may still be too high for people with health problems or those who are elderly. Always consult your doctor for advice pertaining to your personal alcohol consumption).

Photo: © iStockphoto.com, Dirk Freder

145

Be accountable to yourself: begin a journal. Keeping a record of your alcohol consumption will help you in determining how much you really drink, and where you are most likely to drink too much, and with whom. This is strictly for your own information and does not need to be shared with anyone except at your own discretion. You should keep your journal for three or four weeks to give yourself a good idea of any patterns in your drinking. It will reveal both the good and the bad and help you on your way to obtaining your goal.

After you've kept your journal for three to four weeks, take a look back over it. Notice if:

• You drink more when you are alone.
• You drink more when you are with people.
• You drink more with certain people.
• Your drinking makes you late for your job.
• You drink more when you are angry.
• You drink more when you are sad.
• You drink more when you feel lonely.
• You forget what you did while you were drinking.

If you find it impossible to stick to your plan after numerous attempts, you may be setting your goal too high. On the other hand, if your goal is realistic and you still cannot seem to reach it, contact your GP and ask for help. Your drinking problem may be out of control and may indicate you are alcohol-dependent. If so, you will need professional help to stop your drinking completely. Also, if your drinking is causing health problems, you may need to stop completely. Your doctor will help you decide if you can safely consume alcohol moderately, or if you need to stop altogether.

Now, you have a goal and you know why you've set your goal to either drink less or stop. Here are a few tips to help you:

• Keep close tabs on your drinking at home.
• Do not bring alcohol into the house or bring very little.
• When you drink, slow down your consumption by eating along with it.
• Follow your alcoholic drink with a non-alcoholic drink such as fruit juice, soda, or water.
• Never drink on an empty stomach.
• Never drink when you are upset.
• Take a break: pick a day or two during the week where you determine to not drink at all.
• Make positive notes in your journal about how you felt on days you did not drink.
• Stay away from people who give you a hard time about your decision not to drink.
• Learn to say 'no' to alcoholic beverages. Telling your drinking friends you have to stop for medical reasons can provide support from unexpected people.
• Join a support group.

Day one

Today is goal setting day! My goal is:

- I will begin on this day.
- I will drink no more than 5 units in one day.
- I will drink no more than 25 units in one week.
- I plan to reach my goal of moderate drinking/abstinence by: My birthday

    If I do not reach my goal by that time, I will simply start over without feelings of guilt or remorse because I know I can do it!

Today, I drank:
2   drink(s) with   Uncle Fred   at Sonny's Pub   at 3 pm
The type of drink(s) I had was/were   2 pints of lager
While drinking, I felt   sad and depressed

          drink(s) with   at   at
The type of drink(s) I had was/were
While drinking, I felt

          drink(s) with   at   at
The type of drink(s) I had was/were
While drinking, I felt

          drink(s) with   at   at
The type of drink(s) I had was/were
While drinking, I felt

Notes to help me improve

Day two

Today, I drank:

          drink(s) with   at   at
The type of drink(s) I had was/were
While drinking, I felt

          drink(s) with   at   at
The type of drink(s) I had was/were
While drinking, I felt

          drink(s) with   at   at
The type of drink(s) I had was/were
While drinking, I felt

          drink(s) with   at   at
The type of drink(s) I had was/were
While drinking, I felt

Notes to help me improve

Risks

What you need to know

If you drink alcohol only occasionally, you may not realise there are still dangers you should be aware of.

Driving and alcohol

Contrary to popular opinion, it doesn't take much alcohol to impair the most cautious driver's skills. Certain driving abilities are impaired by only 0.02% blood alcohol concentration (BAC). (This is more commonly expressed as 20 milligrams of alcohol per 100 millilitres of blood. The legal limit for driving in much of Europe is 50 mg / 100ml, and in the UK 80 mg / 100 ml.)

Let's take, for instance, a man who weighs around 73 kg (11 stone 7 lb). After he drinks two half pints (568 ml) of beer – say 2 units of alcohol – on an empty stomach, he will have a BAC of about 0.04% (40 mg / 100 ml). (The same effect will occur if he drinks two mixed drinks or two small glasses of wine.) This is enough to slow his reaction times, meaning that in an emergency situation he would not respond as quickly as he would have done had he been completely sober. If he has another two halves, his abilities will be impaired even more, even though he may still pass a roadside breath test.

A startling fact is that many young people are choosing their designated drivers poorly. Instead of choosing one person who abstains completely from alcohol, they are simply choosing the one of the group who is the 'least drunk' to drive. This can result in alcohol-related vehicle accidents, including fatalities. Driving and alcohol don't mix. If no one in your group is alcohol-free, your best bet is to call a taxi, no matter how much your friend may insist on driving.

Some young people admit to letting a drinker drive rather than having to face a confrontation. When it comes to safety – yours and your friends' – the confrontation is worth it. Many have regretted letting drunken friends drive after the fact – after the

According to the University of Alberta

'After a decline of alcohol-impaired driving throughout most of the 1990s, a new study shows that driving while intoxicated has increased significantly and researchers believe it is linked to an increase in binge drinking.

Drunk-driving showed a long, slow decline between 1993 and 1997, from 123 million incidents a year to 116 million. But according to a new national survey, from 1997 to 1999 that figure increased by 37 percent to 159 million and that rate continued in 2002.

The survey, published in the May 2005 issue of the American Journal of Preventive Medicine, also found that four out of five episodes of alcohol-impaired driving were reported by people who also reported binge drinking, defined as consuming five or more units on more than one occasion.'

University of Alberta News Release, Dec. 1, 2005 Rise in Incidents Linked to Binge Drinking Increase

friend has perished in a car accident. Then, it's too late. Using a rotating system can be helpful and lead to fewer confrontations. In other words, tonight you may be the designated driver, abstaining from all alcohol. Tomorrow, someone else would be the designated driver, and so on. This way, each person knows ahead of time what is expected of him.

Many binge drinkers admit they consume more than 5 units per binge. Remembering that two units can impair the driving ability of a 73 kg man; just imagine what more than five drinks would do. Obviously, the binge drinker puts not only himself at risk when he drives, but anyone who may cross his path.

According to the University of Chicago Medical Center, the leading cause of death for people between the ages of 18 and 34 is motor vehicle accidents. In a lifetime, thirty percent of Americans will be involved in a car crash related to alcohol consumption.

How dangerous is drinking and driving . . . really?

A driver who has a blood alcohol concentration of 0.10 % (100 mg / 100ml) or greater is seven times more likely to be involved in a fatal car crash than a driver who has not drunk alcohol at all. A driver with a BAC of 0.15 % (150 mg / 100ml) or greater is twenty-five times more likely to be involved in a fatal car crash.

The naked truth

What it all boils down to is: the more you drink the more likely you are to have an accident, from little bumps to a fatal accident. Here's the naked truth.

As stated earlier, a 73 kg person drinking two beers would probably have a BAC of 0.04 % (40mg / 100 ml), below the legal limit for drink-driving but still more likely to have an accident than someone who is completely sober.

What happens if he has two more beers? The likelihood of an accident goes to eleven times more likely that the non-drinker.

What if he has two more beers? Now, he's had a six-pack, and the likelihood of having an accident is forty-eight times higher than the non-drinker, and he has probably reached a BAC of 0.10 % (100 mg / 100 ml).

He's already had a six-pack. Could two more really hurt anyone? Yes. Now his BAC is at 0.15 % and his risk of having an accident while driving is up to 380 times more than that of his non-drinking buddy.

The truth is, if you plan to party, be sure you designate a driver who is utterly and completely sober. Or have some money for a taxi handy. No matter what, do not get behind the wheel of a car if you've been drinking, or ride as a passenger with a driver who is (or could be) drunk.

Alcohol and medicines

Unfortunately, alcohol and some prescription or over-the-counter drugs just don't mix. Always be aware of any warnings on your medications telling you to stay away from alcohol while taking them. More than 150 drugs should not be taken while consuming alcohol. Adverse reactions may occur if warnings are not heeded. For instance, let's say you have hayfever. Chances are you will take an antihistamine to combat it. If so, and you drink alcohol, the drowsy effect caused by the antihistamine could be compounded by the alcohol. This would make driving, operating machinery, etc, quite hazardous.

What about headaches? Let's say you simply have a headache. You take a painkiller, choosing paracetamol, either by name or in one of its many branded forms. If you drink alcohol while taking it, you may be at risk for serious liver damage. Be sure to check with your doctor or pharmacist before combining medications and alcohol, even if you are only taking an over-the-counter remedy. We are accustomed to think of the risks of prescription drugs with alcohol, but not non-prescription drugs. It's important to treat every drug as a risk with alcohol until you know for sure.

Social and legal problems

Heavy drinking puts you at risk of problems with your family members, your friends, your co-workers, and even people you don't know. Some of these problems may be:

- Arguments with your spouse.
- Discord among your relatives.
- Late to work/school.
- Uncomfortable relationships with co-workers.
- Losing your job.
- Involvement in crimes/violence.

Whoa, baby!

No one likes to think of birth defects. However, if you are pregnant and drinking, you are putting your foetus at risk for birth defects. Even if you are trying to get pregnant, you should not be drinking alcohol. Generally, it takes a while before an expectant mother realises she is pregnant. Children exposed to alcohol before birth may experience lasting learning difficulties and behavioural problems. Most serious is foetal alcohol syndrome or FAS. This causes the child to have severe physical, mental, and behavioural problems. While it is unknown if there is a safe amount to drink while pregnant, experts agree that abstaining from alcohol while pregnant is the best choice.

Heavy drinking in the long-term

There are problems that occur in a short period of time and problems that occur over a longer period of time. Some of those that occur with long-term heavy drinking are liver disease, heart disease, cancer, and pancreatitis. Unfortunately for women, they may develop alcohol-related problems more quickly than their male counterparts.

Heavy drinking, when it's long-term, increases the risks of serious health problems. Millions of people suffer from liver disease that is alcohol-related. Almost every organ in your body feels the effects of alcohol. A complication that some heavy drinkers develop is hepatitis. This is an inflammation of the liver that causes symptoms such as fever, pain in the abdomen, and yellowing of the skin and eyeballs. The urine also develops a much stronger yellow colour than normal. If a person with hepatitis continues to drink, he may die. However, if he chooses to stop drinking, the disease may be reversed.

Another effect alcohol may have on the liver is cirrhosis. This is scarring of the liver. If the person with cirrhosis refuses to stop drinking, he may need a liver transplant (if available) if his

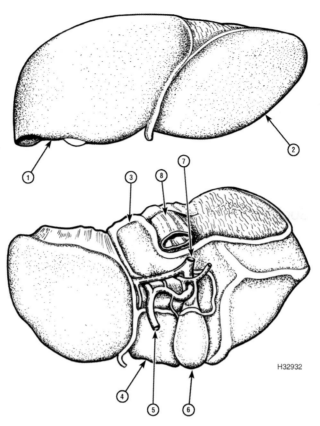

The liver
1 Right lobe
2 Left lobe
3 Caudate lobe
4 Quadrate lobe
5 Hepatic artery
6 Gall bladder
7 Portal vein
8 Inferior vena cava

H32932

condition becomes life threatening. Cirrhosis, unlike hepatitis, is not reversible. However, if the heavy drinker quits drinking, his chances of survival will most likely improve.

People who have Hepatitis C are more prone to liver damage by alcohol than are those who are healthy. If you are diagnosed with Hepatitis C, your best decision would be to quit drinking completely.

Chronic pain, diarrhoea, and unexplained weight loss in a heavy drinker may be an indication that the pancreas is inflamed. Pancreatitis can cause severe abdominal pain or even death. Normally, the pancreas plays a role in regulating the blood sugar levels by producing insulin. It also helps in digestion. Once pancreatitis is diagnosed, the drinker should take steps to eliminate any alcohol from his diet.

Men in their late forties and post-menopausal women are at increased risk for heart attacks. Moderate drinking may actually have beneficial effects for these people. However, once moderate drinking turns into heavy drinking – long-term – the risk for heart disease, high blood pressure, and stroke is greater than if they had never drunk alcohol at all.

The Big C. Most of the time when we think of cancer, we think of smoking as being the greatest risk. However, long-term alcohol consumption can increase the risk of certain kinds of cancer: mouth, throat, larynx, oesophagus, breast, colon, and rectum cancers.

Obviously, the above chronic diseases are reason enough to cut back on drinking if you are a heavy drinker. If you've begun experiencing symptoms, be sure to see your GP immediately as some of these problems can be treated. He will talk to you about your health and suggest ways to curb your drinking.

Could this be you?

The following accounts are examples of what you or your alcohol-dependent loved ones may have experienced. Do any of these seem familiar to you?

The last time I was drunk

Three years ago, at 8 pm, I was on my way to get drunk. Oh, you wouldn't have suspected me of that then. I had been attending Alcoholics Anonymous meetings for quite some time. In fact, just minutes before, I had left an AA meeting. It had been held at a church. I wandered towards my car, one of the last ones to leave. Getting into my car, I noticed to a greater extent what I had noticed during the meeting. My skin was crawling; I needed a drink. It wasn't like I had anywhere else to go. No one was waiting for me at home. I was single. I really didn't like the idea of going home to a dark empty flat. I used that as an excuse to head towards the pub instead of turning for home. I told myself that I would only drink one, just enough to calm my jittery nerves. One drink led to two, which led to three, which led to who knows how many more.

By the time I arrived home, I was more than just a little drunk. I felt like a total failure. The next morning I woke up, totally disgusted at myself and wanting to die. I had one hell of a hangover, including nausea, headache, and dizziness. I didn't want to see or talk to another human being and I cursed the sunlight peeking through the curtains.

Somehow, despite my guilt and shame, I managed to attend the next AA meeting. While I had thought my weeks of sobriety were a total sham, someone mentioned that they were an accomplishment, that I shouldn't worry about it, and all I needed to concentrate on was today. I set my goal right then: No drinking, just for today. Many 'todays' later, I can say I have been sober for three years now.

Sober but nowhere near perfect

I've been sober for several years, but I'm nowhere near perfect. I could have the perfect life – I have a great husband who's stood by me – but I still mess things up, even without alcohol. Today we had a disagreement. It was a silly little thing, but it pissed me off. Now, I'm too proud to go and apologise. So we sit in separate rooms, me with my journal, and him with his reading.

I guess I'm sulking, having a little pity party for me. It's like PMS on steroids. I don't really know why I snapped at him today. Everything was going fine until then. We were in a restaurant, having a conversation. I snapped then at his defensiveness, resorted to silence. The drive home was so uncomfortable, but I refused to apologise. Let him give in first! If the truth be told, looking back, I can see how it was my fault, not his. He was only reacting to my outburst. In two more hours I'll be 7 years away from my last drink . . . sober, but nowhere near perfect.

A step forward

Today I was baptised. Somehow I felt it was the right thing to do on my road to recovery. To me, it's like the 13th step in a 12-step programme. I grew up with the church and it's natural for me to return to my roots. I let alcohol take me away for a while, but now I feel like I'm 'back home,' just where I belong. I can't really explain it in intellectual terms. I just know, for me, it was the right thing to do. It's like a symbol of a promise between God and me. A promise that I will live each day in recovery, one day at a time, one step forward.

Sober but not quite 'there'

The loss of an old friend can bring sad and sorry consequences, particularly when that 'old friend' is The Bottle. Some drinkers never quite get through the grieving process of saying goodbye to their old friend. Some never get over their anger.

For years, alcohol has been their best buddy. When people failed them, The Bottle was always there – ready, willing, and able to chase away their cares. It was reliable. If The Bottle were nowhere to be found in the house, it was simply hanging out down the street at the corner pub or off licence. Once found, the drinker's friend would happily accommodate him whether he chose to entertain at the pub or at home. Unlike people, The Bottle never let him down, never turned against him, never argued with him, was always accommodating. The Bottle was there in the sad times, the bad times, and the party times. Often, it was there during the loneliest of times, too.

However, after a while, The Bottle turned on him. It wasn't quite the good friend it had claimed to be. In fact, it was becoming costly to keep The Bottle as a friend. It became demanding, causing all kinds of withdrawal symptoms when it wasn't invited in. The Bottle also cost the drinker his family, his friends, his health, and his job. In the end, The Bottle was all the drinker had left.

Soon, The Bottle didn't look so good anymore. The drinker decided it was time to give up his good buddy. However, making the decision and carrying through with it wasn't that easy. Grieving for The Bottle set in and soon the drinker was experiencing denial, anger, bargaining, depression, and finally acceptance.

Sadly, some drinkers never quite make it to the acceptance stage. Often, The Bottle wins and the recovered drinker is never quite able to free himself successfully from its clutches. Rather than living successful sober lifestyles, the people who never make it to acceptance may be angry and resentful at 'having' to have made a change in their lives.

Choose wisely

Another Idea . . .

Drinking moderately or not at all is a noble goal. Thus far, you have been focusing on your drinking or not drinking. You have been keeping tabs on yourself and finding out what induces you to drink and what doesn't. You've probably seen some of your weaknesses as well as some of your strengths in your drinking patterns.

Here is another idea in helping you to achieve success in your drinking. Think about what you would like to do.

- What would you like to spend your time and money on instead of alcohol?
- Do you enjoy going to nice restaurants?
- What about taking the kids to the cinema?
- How long has it been since you've played your favourite sport?
- How long has it been since you've seen your favourite team play?

Shock absorbers . . .

Just as your vehicle needs shock absorbers to stabilise it over the humps in the road, you may need support to help you over the humps of life when cutting back on alcohol. It may not be easy to reach your goal. In fact, some days it may be quite difficult. There are several avenues to consider when seeking support:

- Family members and friends who are supportive.
- Online support groups.
- Community support groups.

The truth of the matter . . .

Let's face it . . . most people do not quit drinking all at once. Often, cutting down on alcohol is a lot like cutting back on food. When you're dieting, it isn't easy to say no to tempting pastries or to 'eat just one.' Likewise, when you're watching your alcohol consumption, there will be times when you must face temptations. And there may be times when you actually give in to temptation. However, realise it's okay to fail as long as you pick yourself up and try again. If you don't reach your goal with your first efforts, try again . . . and again, if need be. Your 'shock absorbers' can be quite helpful when it comes to trying again to reach your goal. Your journal can be a big help also. Use whatever tools work for you. Once you reach your goal, you can pat yourself on the back, and be proud of your accomplishment.

Never give up!

Think what else you could spend all that drinking money on

Contacts

5T Consulting: 1-2-1 Solutions
137 Harley Street
London
W1G6BG
Tel: 0207 725 0528
Fax: 01444 245859
Mobile: 07711083507
Email: info@5tconsulting.net
Website: www.5tconsulting.net

Addiction Today
Website has a list of treatment
centres.
Website:
www.addictiontoday.org

Acorn House
58 Albert Road
Levenshulme
Manchester
M19 2AB
Tel: 0161-248-6409
Fax: 0161-248-6996
E-mail:
acorn.house@btconnect.com
Website: www.adas-uk.org

ADAS (Alcohol & Drug
Abstinence Service)
483 Buxton Road
Great Moor
Stockport
Cheshire
SK2 7HQ
Tel: 0161 484 0000
Fax: 0161 484 0011
Email: manager@adas-uk.org
Website: www.adas-uk.org

Addiction Recovery Centre
20 Landport Terrace
Portsmouth
Hampshire
PO1 2RG
Tel: 0800 6199 349
Email: info@arcproject.org.uk
Website:
www.arcproject.org.uk

Al-Anon – for the families of
alcohol abusers.
Website:
www.al-anonuk.org.uk

Alcoholics Anonymous
Website: www.alcoholics-
anonymous.org

Alcohol Concern
Website:
www.alcoholconcern.org.uk

Alcohol Screening
Website:
www.alcoholscreening.org

ANA Treatment Centres
161 Elm Grove
Southsea
Hampshire PO5 1LU
Tel: 023 9283 7837
Fax: 023 9285 1966
Email:
anatcemail@yahoo.co.uk
Website:
www.anaaddictions.co.uk

ARA (Addiction Recovery
Agency)
King's Court
King Street
Bristol BS1 4EE
Tel: 0117 930 0282
Fax: 0117 929 4810
Email:
info@addictionrecovery.org.uk
Website:
www.addictionrecovery.org.uk

Bosence Farm Community Ltd
69 Bosence Road
Townshend
Hayle
Cornwall
TR27 6AN
Tel: 01736 850006
Fax: 01736 851063
Email: info@bosencefarm.com

The Bridges
128 Holderness Road
Hull
HU9 1JP
Tel: 01482 588454
Fax: 01482 588455
Email: info@thebridges.org.uk
Website: www.rapt.org.uk

Broadreach
465 Tavistock Road
Plymouth, Devon PL6 7HE
Tel: 01752 790000
Fax: 01752 785750
Email: enquiry@
broadreach-house.org.uk
Website: www.broadreach-
house.org.uk

Broadway Lodge
Oldmixon Road
Weston-super-Mare
Avon BS24 9NN
Tel: 01934 812319
Fax: 01934 815381
Email: admissions@
broadwaylodge.org.uk
Website:
www.broadwaylodge.org.uk

Capio Nightingale Hospitals
11-19 Lisson Grove
London NW1 6SH
Tel: 0800 783 0594
Fax: 020 7724 9440
Email:
veronica.moss@capio.co.uk
Website: www.capionightingale
hospitals.co.uk

ChildLine
Website: www.childline.org.uk

Closereach
Longcause
Plymouth, Devon PL7 1JB
Tel: 01752 348348
Fax: 01752 347555
Email: admin@
closereach.eclipse.co.uk
Website: www.broadreach-
house.org.uk

Clouds House
East Knoyle
Salisbury
Wiltshire
SP3 6BE
Tel: 01747 830733
Fax: 01747 830783
Email: admin@clouds.org.uk
Website: www.clouds.org.uk

Cottonwood London
78 Wimpole Street
London W1G 9RX
Tel: 020 7486 6222
Fax: 020 7486 2123
Email: info@cottonwood.ltd.uk
Website:
www.cottonwood.ltd.uk

Diana Princess Of Wales
Treatment Centre
Gimingham
Norfolk NR11 8ET
Tel: 01263 722344
Fax: 01263 722455
Email: dianatc@nascr.net
Website:
www.adapt-online.com

Drug And Alcohol Foundation
18 Dartmouth Street
London SW1H 9BL
Tel: 020 7233 0400
Fax: 020 7233 0463
Email: admin@daf-london.com

Farr House
23-24 Farr Street
Avonmouth
Bristol BS11 9JR
Tel: 0117 9048994
Fax: 0117 9074038
E-mail:
farr_house@blueyonder.co.uk

Focus 12
82 Risbygate Street
Bury St Edmunds
Suffolk IP33 3AQ
Tel: 01284 701702
Fax: 01284 704060
Email: info@focus12.co.uk
Website: www.focus12.co.uk

Gilead Foundations
Risdon Farm
Jacobstowe
Okehampton
Devon EX20 3AJ
Tel: 01837 851240
Fax: 01837 851520
Email: admin@gilead.org.uk
Website: www.gilead.org.uk

Godden Green Clinic
Godden Green
Sevenoaks
Kent TN15 0JR
Tel: 01732 763491
Fax: 01732 763160
Email: rikmullender@
cygnethealth.co.uk
Website: www.cygnethealth.co.uk

Health A to Z
Website: www.healthatoz.com

Hebron House
12 Stanley Avenue
Thorpe Hamlet
Norwich NR7 0BE
Tel: 01603 439905
Fax: 01603 700799
Email: info@hebrontrust.org.uk
Website: www.hebrontrust.org.uk

Henley House
Four Mills Lane
Fordton
Crediton
Devon EX17 3PR
Tel: 01363 777958
Fax: 01363 777958
Email: henley.house@
addaction.org.uk
Website:
www.addaction.org.uk

Hope House
49 Saltram Crescent
London
W9 3JS
Tel: 020 8969 3587
Fax: 020 8964 8633
Email: hopehouse@
thecdc.org.uk

Isham House
St Andrew's Group of Hospitals
Billing Road
Northampton
NN1 5DG
Tel: 01604 616100
Fax: 01604 635571
Email: bronwenriordan@
cygnethealth.co.uk
Website: www.cygnethealth.co.uk

Life Works Community
The Grange
High Street
Old Woking
Surrey GU22 8LB
Tel: 01483 757572
Fax: 01483 755966
Email: enquiries@
lifeworkscommunity.com
Website:
www.lifeworkscommunity.com

Life Works Duke Street
4 Duke Steet
London W1U 3EL
Tel: 0800 081 0700
(freephone)
Email: enquiries@
lifeworkscommunity.com
Website:
www.lifeworkscommunity.com

Longreach
7 Hartley Road
Plymouth, DevonPL3 5LW
Tel: 01752 788699
Fax: 01752 789980
Email: longreach@eclipse.co.uk
Website: www.broadreach-
house.org.uk

The Meridian Clinic
Brick Barn Hall
Colchester Road
Bluebridge
Halstead
Essex CO9 2EU
Tel: 01787 473332
Fax: 01787 478882
Email: office@
themeridianclinic.com
Website:
www.themeridianclinic.com

Middlegate Lodge
Horncastle Road
Caistor
Lincolnshire LN7 6JG
Tel: 01472 851540
Fax: 01472 859413
Email:middlegate@
btconnect.com
Website: www.middlegate.co.uk

Mount Carmel
12 Aldrington Road, Streatham
London SW16 1TH
Tel: 020 8769 7674
Fax: 020 8696 0412
Email: mountcarmeluk@
yahoo.co.uk
Website:
www.mountcarmel.org.uk

The Nehemiah Project
47 Tooting Bec Gardens
London SW16 1RF
Tel: 020 8769 3444
Fax: 020 8773 7419
Email: enquiries@tnp.org.uk
Website: www.tnp.org.uk

New Ways Clinic
4 Greengate East, New Moston
Manchester M40 0JL
Tel: 0845 466 1400
Fax: 0161 684 7171
Email: info@newwaysclinic.com
Website:
www.newwaysclinic.com

Open Minds
The Estates House
West Cheshire College
Eaton Road, Handbridge
Chester CH4 7ER
Tel: 01244 675909
Fax: 01244 675882
Email:
info@openminds-ac.com
Website:
www.openminds-ac.com

Parentline
Website:
www.parentlineplus.org.uk

Perry Clayman Project –
PCP Luton
31 Rothesay Road, Luton
Bedfordshire LU1 1QZ
Tel: 01582 730113
Fax: 01582 730114
E-mail: info@
perryclaymanproject.org.uk
Website: www.perryclayman
project.org.uk

Positive Parenting
Website: www.parenting.org.uk

Primrose House
9 Ainger Road
Primrose Hill
London NW3 3AR
Tel: 020 7722 3609
Email: primrosehouse@
btconnect.com
Website:
www.primrosehouse.org.uk

Priory Group
Website:
www.prioryhealthcare.co.uk

Promis
10 Kendrick Mews
South Kensington
London SW7 3HG
Tel: 020 7581 8222
Fax: 020 7581 8515
Email: s.leigh@promis.co.uk
Website: www.promis.co.uk

The Providence Projects
Henley Court
32 Christchurch Road
Bournemouth BH1 3PD
Tel: 01202 555000
Fax: 01202 555100
Email: info@
providenceproject.org
Website:
www.providenceproject.org

Raising Kids
Website:
www.raisingkids.co.uk

Ravenscourt
15 Ellasdale Road
Bognor Regis
West Sussex
PO21 2SG
Tel: 01243 862157
Fax: 01243 867126
Email:
info@ravenscourt.org.uk
Website:
www.ravenscourt.org.uk

Recovery Man
Website:
www.recovery-man.com

Rivendell Healthcare
1 Hanway Place
London
W1T 1HA
Tel: 020 7636 0366
Fax: 020 7323 1715
E-mail:
rivendell10@btconnect.com
Website:
www.rivendellhealthcare.org.uk

The Samaritans
Tel: 08475 909090
E-mail: jo@samaritans.org
Website: www.samaritans.org

SHARP (Self-Help
Addiction Recovery
Programme)
11 Redcliffe Gardens
Earls Courts
London
SW10 9BG
Tel: 020 7349 5772
Fax: 020 7351 4498
Email: info@thecdc.org.uk
Website: www.thecdc.org.uk

SHARP Liverpool (Self-Help
Addiction Recovery
Programme)
17 Rodney Street
Liverpool
L1 9EF
Tel: 0151 703 0679
Fax: 0151 703 0680
Email:
sharpliverpool@thecdc.org.uk
Website: www.thecdc.org.uk

STEPPS Treatment Centre
Ley Court
Minsterworth
Gloucestershire
GL2 8JU
Tel: 01452 750599
Fax: 01452 750757
Email:
mike@steppsrehab.co.uk
Website:
www.steppsrehab.co.uk

Talk to Frank
Website: www.talktofrank.com

Thurston House
52 Rectory Grove
London
SW4 0EB
Tel: 020 7622 7833
Fax: 020 7498 0663
Email:
thurstonhouse@thecdc.org.uk
Website: www.ttpcc.org.uk

Walsingham House
St James Priory Project
Whitson Street
Bristol
BS1 3NZ
Tel: 0117 929 9100
Fax: 0117 922 5980
Email: sjpriory@yahoo.co.uk
Website: www.stjamespriory
project.org.uk

Western Counselling Services
Website:
www.westerncounselling.com

Glossary of Terms

Some of the words in the glossary will be familiar from everyday use but have particular meanings when used in this book.

A

Abstain – to refrain from drinking.

Abstinence – the practice of abstaining from alcoholic beverages.

Accessible – easily obtained.

Accountable – answerable.

Addictive – dependent on a habit-forming substance.

Adolescence – the period of development between puberty and adulthood.

Adolescent – one going through adolescence.

Age of Consent – the age at which a person is legally competent to give consent, as in sexual relations.

AIDS – acquired immune deficiency syndrome; a serious and sometimes fatal sexually transmitted infection caused by HIV.

Alcohol – an intoxicating drink.

Alcohol Abuse – excessive use of alcohol.

Alcohol Dependence – alcoholism.

Alcohol Tolerance – decreased response to alcohol after long-term use.

Alcoholism – an addiction to alcohol.

Alcohol-related – of or relating to alcohol.

Anorexic – suffering from anorexia or loss of appetite.

Anxiety – worry; nervousness.

Asthma – a chronic respiratory disease that causes chest constriction and coughing in sudden attacks.

Autogenic Therapy – a therapy in which patients are trained in self-induced relaxation.

B

BAC – Blood Alcohol Content.

BBB – blood brain barrier.

Beer – a fermented alcohol beverage.

Behavioural Therapy – psychotherapy that modifies undesirable behaviour responses by substituting new ones.

Betrayal – disloyalty.

Black Out – to lose consciousness; pass out.

C

Cancer – malignant neoplasms (growths) that spread into surrounding tissue.

Carbohydrates – a group of compounds, including sugar and starches, which serve as a major source of energy.

Central Nervous System – the part of the nervous system that consists of the brain and the spinal cord.

Cerebellum – the part of the brain that controls muscle coordination.

Cerebral Cortex – the part of the brain that controls higher brain functions, i.e. sensation, thought, memory.

Chemical Modification – an alteration caused by chemicals such as by drugs or alcohol.

Chronic – lasting for a long duration or continuing.

Clarify – to make clear and easy to understand.
Cognitive – relating to factual knowledge.
Colon – a section of the large intestine.
Coma – deep unconsciousness, sometimes fatal.

D

Deception – sham; con; dishonesty.
Denial – a state of refusing to accept the fact one may be addicted to alcohol.
Dependence – craving; habit; obsession.
Depression – hopelessness; sadness; despair.
Deterioration – decline; weakening.
Diabetes – a metabolic disorder often indicated by excessive urination and thirst.
Diagnosis – analysis; conclusion.
Distillation – the process used to produce spirits from wine or other fermented liquid.
Domestic Violence – violence toward one's spouse or partner.
Drunk – intoxicated; inebriated; smashed.
Dysfunctional Family – a socially-impaired family unit.

E

Eating Disorders – any disorder that involves insufficient or excessive food intake.
Emotional Distress – an emotional disturbance which results from another's conduct.
Endocrine System – the glands that control metabolic activity in the body.
Esophagus – American spelling of oesophagus (q.v.)
Essential – necessary; vital.
Ethanol – ethyl alcohol (commonly referred to as just plain alcohol).

F

FAS – Foetal Alcohol Syndrome.
Fermentation – a process in which yeast is used to convert sugar and water to carbon dioxide and alcohol.
Flammable – explosive; burnable.
Folic Acid – a B vitamin that is essential for cell growth.

G

Gastrointestinal (GI) Tract – tubular passageway from mouth to anus.
Genes – a hereditary unit housing DNA.
Goal – objective; purpose.
GP – General Practitioner.

H

Hard Liquor – US term for high alcoholic content beverage, such as gin or whisky.
Heart Attack – a sudden interruption in normal heart functions.
Heart Disease – a disease of the heart or blood vessels.
High – intoxicated.
HIV – human immunodeficiency virus, the organism which causes AIDS.
Hormone – a blood-borne 'messenger' that regulates growth or metabolism.
Hypertension – high blood pressure.
Hypoglycaemia – a low level of glucose in a person's blood.

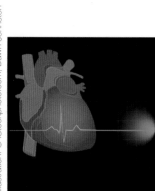

Hypothalamus – the part of the brain that regulates body temperature, metabolic processes, and autonomic activities.

Hypothermia – low body temperature.

I

Illegal Drugs – medications or chemical substances that are bought, sold, or used without a prescription.

Impotence – inability (usually in a sexual context).

Inebriation – drunkenness.

Irritability – sulkiness; ill temper.

J

Jealousy – envy.

Photo: © iStockphoto.com, Tyler Stalman

L

Larynx – the part of the respiratory tract that houses the vocal cords.

Limbic System – interconnected brain structures.

Liver – a large organ that secretes bile, metabolises carbohydrates, fats, and proteins, and eliminates alcohol and other drugs from the bloodstream.

Long-Term – lasting a long time.

Low Self-Esteem – feeling that oneself is not worthy of respect.

M

Magnesium – a metallic element essential for living organisms.

Medication – drugs, either prescription or over-the-counter.

Medulla – the inner part of certain organs.

Metabolise – the way in which the body processes substances such as food or drugs.

Minerals – inorganic elements that are essential to nutrition.

Moderate – sensible; restrained; reasonable.

N

Nausea – queasiness; upset stomach.

Negative – harmful; pessimistic.

Non-alcoholic Drink – a drink that does not contain any alcohol.

Nutrient – a nourishing ingredient in food.

Nutrition – nourishment; food.

O

Obsessive – fixated.

Oesophagus - the passageway down which food travels from the mouth to the stomach.

P

Pancreas – a gland that secretes insulin.

Paranoid – suspicious; mistrustful.

Peer Pressure – the influence of a peer group.

Peers – classmates; equals; social group.

Phobia – fear.

Physical – relating to the body.

Pituitary Gland – a gland located at the base of the brain that is part of the endocrine system.

Positive – definite; optimistic.

Psychological – mental.

Puberty – a stage of development in which an individual becomes capable of sexual reproduction.

Photo: © iStockphoto.com, Mercelo Wain

Photo: © iStockphoto.com, Jan Rihak

R

Reality – actuality; truth.

Recovery – healing from alcohol addiction.

Rectum – the section of the alimentary canal that ends at the anus.

Relapse – to return to drinking alcohol after being abstinent.

Riboflavin – a B vitamin good for skin.

S

Seizures – fits; spasms; convulsions; attacks.

Selenium – a non-metallic element.

Six Pack – perfect abs; also refers to six cans of beer.

Sober – free from the influence of alcohol.

Sobriety – abstinence; being sober.

Social – communal; a group activity.

Spirits - term for high alcoholic content beverage, such as gin or whisky.

Stagger – wobble; walk unsteadily.

STDs – sexually transmitted diseases.

Stroke – a sudden loss of brain function caused by a blockage or rupture of a blood vessel.

T

Therapy – treatment; rehabilitation.

Thiamine – a B vitamin necessary for neural activity.

Toxicity – how poisonous a substance is.

Trauma – pain; suffering; may be physical or psychological.

Treatment – therapy that helps to free the alcoholic from his addiction.

U

Unconscious – out cold; lifeless.

Underage Drinking – drinking alcohol at an age younger than the law allows.

V

Variation – difference.

Vitamin A – Beta Carotene; aids in eyesight, bone and teeth formation; protects mucous membranes.

Vitamin B6 – Pyridoxine; aids in the metabolism of fats and carbohydrates; maintains the central nervous system.

Vitamin B12 – Cobalamin; helps prevent anaemia; needed for calcium absorption; gives energy.

Vitamin C – Ascorbic acid; a major antioxidant; helpful for teeth, gum, and bone health and may ward off the common cold.

Vitamin D – improves absorption of Calcium; essential for bones and teeth; good for the central nervous system and heart.

Vitamin E – supplies oxygen to the blood that retards cellular aging due to oxidation.

Vitamin K – a vitamin that promotes blood clotting.

Vomit – regurgitate; puke.

Vulnerable – susceptible; weak, defenceless.

W

Wine – an alcoholic beverage made from fruit, usually grapes.

Withdrawal – the adjustment of discontinuing an addictive substance.

Z

Zinc – a metallic element essential to plants and animals.